issue one: evangelism

issue one: evangelism

Edited by
Rueben P. Job
and
Harold K. Bales

1908 Grand Avenue, Nashville, Tennessee 37203

Library of Congress Catalog Card Number: 70-120777
© 1970 by Tidings, 1908 Grand Avenue, Nashville, Tenn. 37203
All rights reserved. E169B:370

Contents

Introduction

Evangelism resists an easy definition. When an attempt is made at any simple description, the concept suffers and one is tempted to say: "But evangelism is *more* than that." Evangelism is a continuing, changing, living union of many elements.

The central element in Christian evangelism must be *content*, the gospel of Jesus Christ. This gospel which illuminates Christian history and the current human situation provides a lively encounter with the truth of existence and a compelling motivation for witness to that truth.

A necessary element in evangelism is *commitment*. Evangelism demands the involvement of persons whose understanding of the gospel has resulted in a willingness to risk the hazards of a pilgrimage of faith. Persons committed to the source of the gospel constitute a vital part of the dynamics of evangelism.

Evangelism includes *proclamation*. It is proclamation motivated by concern for the needs of persons and the conviction that the gospel provides hope for human life. It is proclamation that is both word and action.

Evangelism is *doing* as well as believing. It is an event in which words and deeds become alive with a witness to the salvation that is possible though the world seems to be falling apart at the seams.

Content, commitment, and proclamation are a dynamic mixture, unified and empowered by the Spirit of God and set afoot in today's world to bear witness to the truth. This is evangelism —a "happening," an event. It is a continuing, changing event where exciting things can take place:

1. Conversion of the old, irrelevant things that destroy life can result. A new creation is a possibility.

2. Renewal of essential elements of life can happen. The traditions of the Christian faith can become meaningful for modern man.

3. Disclosure of God in new ways is inevitable as God works in history.

4. Openness to the future becomes an exciting possibility when it is affirmed that the future belongs to God.

5. Reason for existence in the turbulent present is provided as persons are called to faith commitments.

Evangelism is an event and these are some results of that

"happening" where medium and message unite in the context of a watching, listening, doubting world.

This book seeks to provide a focus on the primary issue for the church in the 1970's—evangelism. Here is a gathering of content, commitment and proclamation. The content of evangelism—the gospel—is discussed as theological concepts by Christian scholars. Commitment is affirmed by each of these authors in their personal life and in their contributions to this volume. Proclamation is present as each writer offers his interpretation of the Word—some articles are, in fact, sermons. And the practical, concrete aspect of evangelism is affirmed by articles with creative suggestions for the *how* of bearing witness to the truth. A uniting of content, commitment, proclamation—this is evangelism, issue one!

1

Rethinking the Great Commission in an Age of Revolution

by ELMER GEORGE HOMRIGHAUSEN

I
THE HEART OF CHRISTIANITY

Christians should always be thinking about the faith by which they live. This is the way to keep the wonder and the vitality and the meaning of the faith alive. It is the way to keep it from becoming a habit or a form. And it is the way to probe more deeply into the Christian faith and grow into the maturity which it offers.

However, there are times in history when Christians are confronted with a critical situation and are forced to re-think their faith. This is such a time. Two dangers always confront the Christian faith: one is that it relates itself so closely with its past and becomes a museum piece, and the other is that it becomes so modern that it diffuses itself into a secular faith. That is, it may try to preserve itself by holding on to its past traditions, or it may try to modernize itself by becoming secular. Today, this tension between the old and the new is causing much unrest in the churches. As a result, Christians are being forced to rediscover the essentials of the Christian faith.

It has been said that we are living in a time of Exodus. The book by that name describes the liberation of the Israelites from their Egyptian slavery. On that fateful night of freedom, they were told to travel lightly, and to take with them only such things as they could carry. They were not to be encumbered with excess

Elmer George Homrighausen is Charles R. Erdman Professor of Pastoral Theology at Princeton Theological Seminary. He holds degrees from Lakeland College, Princeton Theological Seminary, Butler University, and the University of Dubuque. He has served as a distinguished pastor and teacher, and is the author of several books and articles on religious themes. The article included here was the Belk Lecture Series of 1968, delivered at St. Giles Presbyterian Church, Richmond, Virginia. This article is reprinted with the permission of the author and St. Giles Presbyterian Church.

baggage. Such is the situation today. The churches are called
upon to strip down and move into the future with the bare
essentials of faith.

The great historian, Adolph Harnack, wrote a book entitled
What is Christianity? in which he maintained that soon after
the Christian faith was launched it began to change its simple
nature into something very complex. While we do not subscribe
to his thesis that the early church altered the faith from one
centering in the religion of Jesus to one centering in the religion
about Jesus, it is possible that we have tended to substitute for
the simplicity of the gospel the complexity of an institutional
Christianity.

This critical situation is not new for the Christian faith. Sometimes it has been interpreted with an emphasis upon doctrine.
Christianity has been called a system of propositions. To be a
Christian is to assent to a set of truths. Now, the Christian faith
centers in truth. Indeed, Jesus Christ is the truth that gives
men the light of the knowledge of themselves and their God.
Jesus came to save men from ignorance, error and superstition,
to make them free in the truth. But there is more to it than
truth. Truth is a fruit; what is the root that produces truth?

Sometimes Christianity has been interpreted with an emphasis
upon conduct. Indeed, Jesus came into the world to make men
good. "By their fruits shall ye know them," said Jesus. But
what produces a good man? Goodness is a fruit; what is the root
of goodness?

And sometimes in history, Christianity has been interpreted
in terms of order and institution. And indeed Christianity has its
sanctuaries, schools, hospitals, publishing houses. It has its
orders and regulations. All these are inevitable fruits. What is
the root of reality and vitality that produces these institutions?

All these are important, but today we must go beyond creed
and code of conduct and institution. What is the heart of the
Christian faith? What gave it birth; what has kept it alive
through changing centuries; what will make it vital today?

Perhaps we have the answer in the words of our text. They
were spoken by Jesus in the Upper Room on the last night of his
life. He was conversing with them about his life and death, and
their future ministry. They were meeting in secret. And he revealed the inmost secret of his purpose to them. He spoke of
himself as the life-giving vine that gives life to the branches.
He made it clear that they must also be servants as he was when
he washed their feet. And he said, "A new age has come. From
now onward, I call you servants no longer . . . I call you friends.
All I have received from my Father I have shared with you

without limit." This is the heart of Christianity! It is God sharing his very life with men. He has broken down the wall that separates servant and master. He has made fellowship possible. God has reconciled the world to himself. God in Christ made us his friends.

This friendship of which Jesus speaks is a precious gift. None deserves it. Its offer is a complete surprise! The New Testament is alive with the sense of joy based upon this gift of God's grace. The Christian message centered in the wonder of "God and sinners reconciled," and "Peace on earth among men of good will."

John put it, "Herein is love, not that we loved God, but that God loved us and sent his son to be the propitiation for our sins." "While we were yet sinners, Christ died for us." The wall of separation has been broken down. A new relationship has been established between God and man. Jesus Christ is our "peace," is the way the writer of the letter to the Ephesians states it.

And the initiative was taken by God. "You did not choose me, but I chose you, and ordained you, that you should bear fruit."

The New Testament from beginning to end speaks of "the unspeakable gift," "the excellent knowledge," "the unsearchable riches."

This is the essence of the gospel, or good news. It is the heart of the Christian faith. It is the central concern of the church to know, to love, to proclaim, and to teach this gospel. This is what makes a church a church. Without it, a church lacks the spirit of joy and mission and hope. The renewal of the church is not to be found in gimmicks and spiked-up programs and adaptations to the secular mentality; rather, it is in rediscovering afresh the wonder and the glory and the power of the gospel.

Perhaps the churches have heard the gospel so often that it has become deadly dull through familiarity. In some parts of the Christian world churches have been rudely shaken out of their complacency through the hostile environment in which they must live. In some parts of the Christian world, Christians have become aware of their comfortable affluence and are uneasy about themselves and their mission. God is prodding his people to think seriously about the gospel in a time of trouble.

An experience comes to mind which is related to one of Princeton's most illustrious citizens, Dr. Albert Einstein. He was a good neighbor. Though he was great, there was about him a simplicity that was disarming. He was a refugee and a displaced person. He lost everything under the Hitler tyranny. He came to the United States, and without bitterness in his heart, started life anew. He was a mystic; as a great scientist, the universe for

him was full of wonder. And he loved little children and music
and nature. He was a good friend of Princeton Seminary. One
thing he did I shall never forget. There were other refugees
from central Europe who came to the United States: statesmen,
educators, scientists. Many were past middle life and they approached their future in a strange land with little hope. They
came to New York. From time to time, Dr. Forrell, who be-
friended these refugees, brought them to Princeton for a day's
visit. And without their knowledge, I had them meet Dr. Einstein
in Miller Chapel. When they saw Dr. Einstein, they could not
believe their eyes. Would the great man take time to visit with
them? Indeed he did. He spoke to them encouragingly. He gave
many his autograph. He shook their hands. They never forgot
the occasion! Why? Because greatness had visited them, their
situation seemed to change.

There is quite a world of difference between Dr. Albert Einstein and Jesus Christ. But this is the way the early Christians
felt about Jesus: "The Son of God has visited us," they shouted.
"And since he honored us with his presence, and he is for us,
life takes on a new possibility. From now onward . . . we are
no longer slaves; we are friends of God through the Prince of
Life."

This friendship of which Jesus speaks is a powerful force for
the changing of human personality. It sets up a relationship or
an encounter with persons that makes life new. There is no power
like that of the influence of person on person in the reshaping
of human life.

This has been made evident in our generation through the
cult of personality. I do not mind the cult of personality provided
the person at the center of the cult is worthy and is life-redeem-
ing. One thinks of the power of Churchill and Roosevelt and
John F. Kennedy and Eisenhower. Yes, and of Adolf Hitler and
Josef Stalin! I have seen a newspaper photo of John F. Kennedy
in the homes of people in Asia and Africa. I have come across
a John F. Kennedy Book Store in a street in Madras. Never
discredit the power of personality!

In a recent study to determine whether students change their
ideals during their college education, it was found that few were
affected by the courses they pursued; some changed their ideals
because of the powerful influence of professors on campus with
whom they associated.

God reveals himself in nature, history, and the conscience of
man. But, as the letter to the Hebrews puts it, he revealed
himself at last through a son, a person. "The word became flesh
and we beheld him full of grace and truth." And Jesus said,

"He that has seen me has seen the Father." God's strategy for reaching men with his friendship is through his Son, the Friend of Man.

In the New Testament, the process by which persons become new is through a relationship with the Person, Jesus Christ. In and through him, people meet God and engage in a dialogue of redemption. This process of revelation and responding faith is the way to the life that is "abundant" and "eternal." Jesus does two things to those he meets: he encourages them by his grace into the new self that is in him, and he shames and judges them out of their old selves. On the one hand, his grace saves, and on the other hand his righteousness condemns. To find true life is to be related to Jesus Christ, Friend, through decision and continuing commitment. The Christian life is one that is lived in a continuing relation with Jesus Christ. The apostle Paul put it simply, "For me to live—is Christ."

The power of Jesus Christ has gone abroad in the earth. In nearly all nations there are those who have responded to his friendship and who are seeking to grow up into the full implications of that new relationship. One sees him at work among the Bataks of Indonesia, among the aboriginals of mountainous Taiwan, among the Kikuyas of Kenya, among the Indians of the Amazon valley. These Christian communities were brought into being not by a set of doctrines, a code of ethics, or an ecclesiastical institution. Rather, they are the product of the powerful influence of the Person of Jesus Christ, mediated through persons who in turn were influenced by this Friend. The whole Christian community is a network of friends who influence each other. And at the heart of this community of friends is the great Friend: Jesus Christ.

The church's major commission is to "preach" this Jesus Christ. This means to magnify and celebrate him. It means to make him known through life and word and fellowship and service. It means to bring about that creative and life-changing encounter which will result in discipleship and growth into the maturity of life that he has come to share.

This friendship of which Jesus speaks is a creative social force. It is strong and responsible good will. After Jesus had washed the disciples' feet, he put the question to them, "Do you know what I have done to you?" They were no doubt stunned into silence by this astonishing act of servitude on the part of the one whom they respected as master. Then Jesus answered, "You call me master and lord; and you say well; for so I am. If I, your lord and master, have washed your feet, you also ought to wash one another's feet. For I have given you an example, that you should do as I have done to you. Verily, verily, I say unto you, the servant is not greater than his lord; neither is he that is sent greater than he that sent him."

Jesus Christ is the center of a company of servants. They cohere in him, and from him they have learned to serve one another.

The question is often asked these days when the church is being criticized, "What is the church?" And the usual answer is that the church is an institution or an organization. However, the friendship that is in Jesus Christ clearly indicates that the church is people. It is a company of friends who celebrate the friendship of God in Jesus Christ, and who practice that friendship towards each other. They give each other the hand of encouraging friendship; they shed for each other "the sympathizing tear." They support one another in grief; they share themselves and their abundance with each other. They want their children to know this friendship of God and to learn about its power, history and prospect. They find in his friendship the dynamic for Christian unity.

However, this friendship is not to be kept within the company of Christians; it is to be demonstrated and shared with the world. It is the secret of social service and action. It is the source of concern and action in social conditions that make this friendship possible. In a world of tension, strife, and even violence, this friendship is the only antidote that can temper the evil situation with strong goodwill and the spirit of reconciliation.

Christians are known by different names. Some are called Presbyterians, others Lutheran, and still others Methodist, Episcopalians, Reformed, Pentecostals, and so forth. Only a few groups are known by biblical terms: Disciples, Brethren, Friends. These historical designations had their appeal in their time. They still carry great historical traditions. However, the time has come when Christians and churches should be less concerned about historical designations and more concerned about present realities. Whatever the Christian community may be or become, it is certainly one in which this strong friendship of God that was in Jesus Christ is a reality.

Little wonder, then, that the apostle Paul regarded love as the greatest thing in the world. In I Corinthians 13, he wrote that one could speak with tongues of men and of angels, but that if he did not have love, his oratory, however brilliant, would be like sounding brass or a tinkling cymbal. One could have faith so as to remove mountains, but if it lacked love, it had no lasting or attracting power. If he discovered the mysteries of God—perhaps split the atom—and possessed all knowledge, but had not love, he was nothing. And if he gave all his goods away and offered himself as a martyr for a cause, but did not have love, it profited nothing!

Deep, understanding, human friendship that is rooted in the eternal Friendship of God is indeed a precious gift, a personality-changing power, and a vital social force.

And Jesus enforced his appeal by adding a postscript: This is my commandment; that ye love one another as I have loved you!

II
RETHINKING THE GREAT COMMISSION

CONCEPT

The Great Commission brings to a ringing conclusion Matthew's account of the historical career of Jesus Christ. Some scholars have questioned its place in the original manuscript. They believe that it may have been added by an honest editor, and accepted by the early church as an authentic part of the apostolic witness to the Christ-event.

However, even if the Commission is not an integral part of Matthew's Gospel, and even if Jesus never gave this mandate in the exact words of Matthew 28: 18-20, it rings true to the gospel record and to the mind and ministry of Jesus Christ. These words reflect the genuine and authentic experience of the earliest Christians. And they have been sanctioned by centuries of accepted use.

As Dr. George Buttrick puts it in *The Interpreter's Bible,* the gospel ends with (1) a claim, (2) a commission, and (3) a promise. Christ claims to be Lord of life and death and history. He has the integrity and therefore the right to commission his followers to claim men's allegiance among all nations and to the end of time. He is the true Word about human nature, about its restoration and fulfillment, about man's historical destiny in the purpose of God, and about the "saving" relations among men and nations by which they may have life abundant and eternal on this good earth—and beyond. Therefore—Go!

The Commission is threefold: disciple; baptize; teach! Here we confront the concept involved in the Commission, about which this lecture is concerned. Each aspect of the task is wide and weighty with meaning. To "disciple" is to make the claim of Christ's authority meaningful and persuasive. The aim is acceptance and enlistment. This is no easy assignment. Nor is it well understood in our time. To baptize into the "name" is to be initiated into the character and cause of Jesus Christ as person and as nucleus of a new humanity. This "rite of passage" is crucial in the life of the Christian enterprise, and it needs to be rescued from its cultural and religious formalism. And to teach in the true sense of the term is to lead the enlisted and the baptized into the full ramifications of discipleship in intellectual, social, ethical and devotional maturity and responsibility.

General Concern

There is general concern in most of the churches about their loss of apostolic nerve. This is evident to some extent in the statistics of some denominations. One large Protestant communion with over three million members lost twenty-five thousand members during the past year. To be sure, statistics cannot be used to measure the spiritual vitality of a church; in some instances, losses may indicate that a denomination has tightened up its standards of membership and cleaned up its roll.

However, the total situation does not lend itself to such an optimistic evaluation of the state of the churches. According to a national poll which is quite representative, popular opinion believes that the churches have lost a great deal of influence in society in recent years.

Combined with this loss of influence of the church in society is the much larger problem of Western culture or so-called Christendom, in general, and American culture in particular. A gradual erosion of Christian commitment and character has been taking place in Christendom to such an extent that some observers call it "post-Christian." Whether it was ever Christian may be debated, but that it is no longer what it once was, is quite evident. The cultural support of Christianity in the West has been gradually disintegrated until the churches today find themselves exposed and alone. The Christian church is no longer "established" by cultural support. A cultural pluralism has developed in which Christianity is no longer the dominant or protected faith. This process started many years ago; in fact, at the beginning of the modern era. France became the first western secular state, and Russia has since become the first atheistic community. But even in countries like Sweden where over ninety-five percent of the population belongs to one national church, and Christianity is integrally related to national education and culture, this process of desacralization has taken place through science and technology.

In face of this new situation, the churches are confronting a new secular climate and technological environment. Western culture is no longer a carrier of the Christian faith; the churches are now more and more on their own. It is now necessary for them to become true churches in a strange situation. As a result, the churches are engaged in active and restless theological reflection. In such a time of doctrinal fluidity, ecumenical relations, and social change, one may well expect unrest in the churches, and even a measure of uncertainty in matters of faith and practice. This uncertainty has affected the apostolic obedience of the church to the Great Commission. Most of the churches are on a plateau in evangelistic effort. Much time is being spent on studies in evangelism, perhaps with a view to determining afresh what the nature of the gospel is, and what it is intended to produce in the way of a style of life. And if there is a hesitation on these crucial matters, there will be hesitation in fulfilling the apostolic mandate.

Evangelistic programs are practically at a standstill in most denominations. Doubt is expressed about older methods of evangelism: mass meetings, visitation evangelism, person-to-person evangelism, and campaigns for church membership. And no new methods are proposed to take their place. Criticism of older methods centers largely in their emphasis upon personal salvation and their failure to call persons for commitment to a gospel that aims at the salvation of the whole man: body, mind and spirit, and the salvation of man from all that enslaves him to a sub-human life and prevents him from liberation into his true humanity, personal and social.

There is abroad today an imperious concern about the great social issues of our time. This concern makes an emphasis upon personal salvation almost unethical to many people. Besides, the biblical dimensions of the Lordship of Jesus Christ and the Christian commitment raise serious questions regarding an evangelism that centers only in a personal relationship to Jesus Christ.

This concern is felt in the National Council of Churches. At its last assembly in Miami Beach in December 1966, the general secretary, Dr. Edwin Espey, placed evangelism at the top of a list of priorities which should concern the Council and its affiliated churches. Dr. Billy Graham addressed the Assembly, and also participated in a dialogue on evangelism with the then-secretary, Dr. Colin Williams. That Dr. Graham was invited to address the Assembly, was in itself an indication that the churches were desirous not only to hear him speak, but to carry on a friendly association with him and his association. To be sure, there were disagreements, especially between Dr. Graham and Dr. Williams and their followers! No consensus was reached! In some ways, the disagreements were accentuated. And even

though the Council now subsumes evangelism in one of its major
divisions, the concern for evangelism is kept alive, especially
through summer assemblies and continuing studies on the subject, often in line with the World Council of Churches.

This concern for evangelism has been on the agenda of the
World Council of Churches since its organization in Amsterdam
in 1948. Indeed, the ecumenical movement was inspired by the
apostolic commission of Jesus Christ in Edinburgh in 1910.
Every Assembly since 1948 has had a section devoted to evangelism. Many studies have been made on the subject, which now
include the meaning of baptism, salvation, conversion, and the
missionary structure of the local congregation. The Interna-
tional Missionary Council has been incorporated into the World
Council of Churches to form one of the largest Divisions of the
Council: World Mission and Evangelism. One of the major concerns of the Council has been the renewal of the churches, and
in this concern, the Ecumenical Institute has been a pioneer
force. To indicate the need for a recovery of the apostolic zeal
of the churches in the ecumenical movement, we have but to
refer to one of the most impressive addresses given at the
Uppsala Assembly in 1968 by the secretary-emeritus of the Council, Dr. Visser 't Hooft on the need for motivation in the
ecumenical enterprise. And Dr. John A. Mackay, president emeri-
tus of Princeton Theological Seminary has called for an evangelical revival at this crucial time.

This concern is felt not only in the churches, but in groups
outside the churches as well. Some scientists fear the use of
power by persons who are not committed to Judaeo-Christian
ethical standards. Students of politics call attention to the fact
that democracy is a fragile way by which people govern themselves; if citizens are not intelligent and responsible, the will of
ignorant and irresponsible people may be disastrous. The crisis
in personal and public morality is related to the erosion of a
quality of life which is rooted in commitment to values that
transcend self-interest.

The United States now finds itself in its third historical crisis.
The first was the civil war, the second the great depression, and
the third is the current situation. It is striving toward self-
identity in an unstable world at a time when it is confronted
by a nasty situation in Asia, and an uneasy situation in its
cities. This nation has been called a "confused giant."

The problem which the churches confront in the United States
is that of exercising their prophetic and pastoral roles to this
powerful nation in distress, when they have grown uncertain in
their conception of themselves, the nature of the gospel, and the

way to fulfill their apostolic mission to the country and to the world.

However serious the situation, it is out of difficult times like these that creative possibilities may emerge. It has been said repeatedly that today "everything is up for grabs," by which is meant that everything is being questioned in order to find genuineness and integrity and reality. The Christian and the church should welcome such scrutiny for they have nothing to hide or fear or protect. They are concerned about the truth. And the truth is liberating and inspiring!

Controversial Subject

Why should there be controversy in the churches about the Great Commission? If its mandate is a part of the gospel record, what alternative is there but to obey or disobey it? The claim, the commission, the promise, are not to be argued, but accepted!

Yet, controversy in this matter is not new; it is as old as the Christian community. Every major Christian communion has its own conception as to how the Great Commission is to be fulfilled. This is because they have their ideas as to the nature and scope of the Lordship of Jesus Christ; their ideas as to how persons are to be made disciples of Jesus Christ; their ideas as to the meaning of discipleship; their ideas as to what these disciples are to be taught; their ideas as to the relation of disciples to the world; their ideas as to whether the "end of the age" is the coming of Christ's Kingdom *in* history or *beyond* history. To be sure, ecumenical relations and conversations have made the lines of difference more indistinct, even though the great patterns of apostolic obedience are still with us.

Professor Pieter De Jong reminds us in his interesting volume entitled *Evangelism and Contemporary Theology*, that every one of the great theologians has a theological stance that bears upon the Great Commission. The apostolic commission is interpreted by each in a slightly variant way, whether it is Barth, Brunner, Bultmann, Tillich, Reinhold Niebuhr, or Bonhoeffer. Indeed, the reading of this study in the implications for evangelism of six modern theologians will indicate to the reader why there is fluidity in thinking about the meaning of Christian discipleship today. These theologians have made a profound impression upon the leadership of the church. However, this study will also indicate to the reader the depth and breadth involved in the present controversy. Out of this creative controversy there may come a richer and purer concept of the nature of discipleship in our time.

One of the major controversies now in progress is that between what may be termed the "personal salvationist" and the "social salvationist." This is an oversimplification, to be sure. Those who insist upon the primacy and necessity of personal salvation through repentance and faith in Jesus Christ do not ignore the social aspects of that salvation. Indeed, Dr. Graham has said that every man needs two conversions: one to Jesus Christ, and the other to the world. On the other hand, the social salvationists believe in God's concern for the salvation of the whole man and the whole world of human relationships, and that commitment to this mandate of Jesus Christ involves the individual in a deep personal transformation.

The personal salvationists are critical of the current trend to equate evangelism with social justice. They are fearful that the nature of the Christian faith may be changed into a program of social action for the wellbeing of mankind. This, they feel, is a radical transformation of the gospel that cuts out its heart.

The social salvationists believe that a concentration on the salvation of the individual through a personal relation to Jesus Christ is too individualistic, that it is not commensurate with the gospel's full intention. They hold that God loves the whole world, that he is at work in the world to implement that love, that in Jesus Christ he has released his liberating movement to free men into their true and full humanity. Instead of salvation, they speak of "humanization" as the purpose of God-in-Christ. They interpret Jesus' manifesto in this light. He came to set men at liberty and to free them from their dehumanizing slaveries. God's salvation is a covenant, a world, a global salvation.

It is unfortunate that these two emphases should be placed in such sharp contrast. There is no warrant for this separation in either the Old or New Testaments. And separation of the personal and the corporate is a distortion of Christianity; it fails to grasp the higher and deeper unity of the purpose of God in relation to the meaning and destiny of human life.

However, this controversy is felt in all the denominations, and in the National and World Councils of Churches. It has been said that any attempt to define what obedience to the apostolic commission is in the World Council of Churches would result in a serious division!

Eastern Orthodox Churches, for instance, are fearful of aggressive evangelism. They call it "proselytism" because it is often done by sectarian groups usually from America who "convert" members of Orthodox churches to their "true faith" from what they regard as old and dead churches. This emphasis upon personal conversion and a church of gathered converts runs counter to the whole conception of the church in Orthodoxy.

Here it can be seen that two conceptions of the nature of the Christian life and the church are in conflict. And this is a source of continuing controversy. Were the Orthodox to become more evangelical and introduce the practice of preaching into their own churches, perhaps this conflict would not arise.

To be sure, there has always been controversy about methods of evangelism. Mass evangelism has come in for attack because of its hyperemotionalism, its theological divisiveness, its extra and often anti-church mentality, its coercive and unethical methods, and often its financial irregularities. It is now maintained that this method no longer reaches the outsider. It fosters a type of Christianity that was apropos to a former time. It fosters a Christian experience of a revival type which the convert does not find in the local church when the campaign is finished.

However, there is a place for the people of God to meet to celebrate the gospel in song, sermon and prayer. When shorn of its objectionable theology and methods, and done in unity, and where possible, with Roman Catholics, Pentecostals, and others, it can give great support to Christians, be an occasion for a larger re-commitment, and a witness to the whole community. This method is quite effective among the younger sister churches, and still may be employed with great effectiveness in many areas of the world.

The controversy is also precipitated by the changed situation in which the apostolic mandate is to be exercised. This is a secular age in which the new generation has little understanding of or appreciation for the older framework of theology. This is the "now" generation. The old religious framework does not seem to be compatible with the new outlook. Therefore, an evangelism that is always calling people "back" to the old-time religion, or "out" of this secular world, seems to be a reversion that does not take seriously the present age in which we live.

Another source of controversy is over the meaning of conversion. The personal salvationists make a great deal of the principle that "to change man's heart will lead to social change." This principle is now being challenged. It "ain't necessarily so," say some sincere Christians. And it has not been so always. Dr. Emilio Castro, a Methodist pastor from Uruguay wrote recently, "No such thing as man's heart exists apart from man's relations." He cites the failure of the churches using traditional methods to witness in the secular world. He writes . . . "conversion means that we become aware of a relationship with Jesus Christ, and this means, in time, relationship with our neighbor. It means becoming part of the discipleship of those who serve. The two elements—relation with Jesus Christ and relation with my neighbor—can be distinguished, but they cannot be separated. No relationship with Jesus Christ exists that is not a relationship with our neighbor." In short, he is saying that a personal relationship with Jesus Christ is not first, to be followed by a relationship with the neighbor; instead, they are integrally related. The churches are not to be anti-secular, but rather to see this secular world in its modern development as God's world. We are not to be saved out of this world; rather, we are to become disciples of Jesus Christ in this world, and in this secular age. God is the living God of Abraham, Isaac, and Jacob; the God and Father of our Lord Jesus Christ; the God of Luther and Calvin and Knox; the living God of modern man, atomic energy, and present history. God *is* at work in the world. The "presence" of Jesus Christ in all his redemptive activity has been released into human life and history, and he is at work everywhere. It is the business of the apostolic witness to make known to all nations that God has inaugurated a new order, that it is under way, that the pivotal battle has been won, that we are living between the first and second coming of Christ, and that men are called to make their peace with this God by enlisting in his enterprise through the action of faith and repentance and obedience. The kingdom is in the midst of our secular world with all its problems and issues and promises and tragedies. It is not "up" there, but here—and to come! God's concern is for the liberation of man into his true manhood, personal and social. And the group of persons who know this secret of God and are committed to discipleship in his cause *is the Church.*

The most serious aspects of the controversy, therefore, are raised by Dr. Philip Potter, secretary of the Division of World Mission and Evangelism of the World Council of Churches. He maintains that the "death of God" theologies, religious and cultural pluralism, radical social unrest, and hesitation about the uniqueness of Jesus Christ over against other religions have brought about a failure of nerve among Christians concerning the evangelistic witness. While those who believe in evangelism agree that it is a necessary task, the real controversy now is over the *content* of an older evangelism itself. The fluid state of theology, the misgivings of the churches about an older evangelism, the imperious claim of human social needs, the uncertainty about the uniqueness of Jesus Christ, and the confusion about the nature of the Christian style of life, have brought about a paralysis of evangelistic activity in the churches. There is abroad, even among Christians, a spirit of tolerance about the relation of Christianity to other religions. Christians do not wish to be offensive in pushing the uniqueness of their gospel. So, they interpret Christianity as belief in God, the decent life and the altruistic spirit, a kind of "religion in general." All religions may be the same, and perhaps the best in all of them may be worked into a world religion that would be suitable to the age. The historian, Arnold Toynbee, believes that in a developing unity among peoples of the earth, any stress upon the onlyness or uniqueness of Christianity should be modified or surrendered. Such an interpretation of Christianity cuts the nerve of its distinctive nature and robs it of its right to carry on a creative dialogue with other faiths.

The emphasis today in the churches on the church as *mission* is also involved in this controversy. If the mission of the church is conceived of largely as obedient social action aimed to relieve mankind of its ills, the inner relationship of man and God will be changed, or, minimized. Indeed, the total church is engaged in many tasks as it fulfills its total mission to man and humanity. However, unless the apostolic task is given its rightful place in this mission, the church as mission may be diffused into worthwhile services, but in the process lose its dynamic source and continuing motivation.

If there is uncertainty about the authority of Jesus Christ and the nature of discipleship, there will be uncertainty in obeying the apostolic mandate!

This controversy is to be welcomed. It provides an opportunity for a serious re-appraisal of the deeper meanings and wider implications of discipleship in a new age. This is a time of "creative controversy" in considering the apostolic mandate of Jesus Christ.

Primary Task

Without evangelism, no one becomes a committed Christian, and without evangelism, no one continues to grow into a vital Christian maturity. If this task is not done, the Christian community cannot exist; if it is not done continuously in the Christian community, it may soon degenerate into a formal religious institution.

Jesus Christ made the apostolic witness primary. After his ministry or service to God and man, he said, *Therefore, Go!* His Lordship is the source of this primary responsibility of those who know him. And since he is Lord, the world must be told; it has a right to be informed of this wonderful news. This Charter of Redemption and Freedom cannot be confined by racial, geographical, ethnic or generational boundaries.

Jesus said, "You did not choose me; I chose you . . . that you should go and bear fruit." And one of the fruits is the obedience to this Lord. Human beings did not invent Jesus Christ; nor did they generate the truth, love and right that were in him and which radiated from him.

Nor were the disciples to keep their experience of what had come to them through their association with him to themselves. Standing by and looking up as he ascended, a voice said to them, "Why stand here idle, looking up? This same Jesus will return. Turn your eyes outward towards the world and forward towards his future. Be my witnesses to the ends of the earth." The Christian faith does not end in vision; it issues in obedience to a world commission. The apostolic obligation is primary.

The life and work of the church depends upon the primacy of the apostolic mandate. The outsider has no ordinary way of knowing the gospel except he be brought the message. Discipleship is not self-generated. And even in the life of the Christian congregation, it is impossible to separate the apostolic mandate from the various ministries of the church whether education, pastoral care, worship, or social service and action. The gospel of Jesus Christ must be the constant motivation for *all* the ministries of the church, or they cease to be infused with the dynamic of commitment and re-commitment. Evangelism is not the only ministry of the local congregation but it does come first if it is to exist at all; and it must remain first if it is to keep its sense of commitment alive. This does not mean that every congregation will be seeking to convert its people over and over again! That is a distortion of the Christian enterprise and makes it into a continuous recruiting station without reference to education and training for the issues of the committed life.

The late Professor Karl Heim of Tuebingen once said that when the apostolic dynamic was lessened in the church, it was like throwing the master switch of a great factory that stopped the entire machine. Without the apostolic dynamic, a congregation may be a religious establishment and even a successful institution, but it has lost its soul.

Then, too, the apostolic mandate is primary for sheer pragmatic reasons. The Christian faith is not inherited through the bloodstream. No one becomes a Christian by proxy. God has hermetically sealed each of us off from our neighbors, and it is impossible even for parents who love their children to implant their faith in the souls of their offspring. To become too aggressive in dogmatic instruction may cause the child to "parrot" the faith of his parents, but it is not his own faith. A recent pamphlet that came to hand asked, "Will your grandchildren be Christians?" As a grandparent, I was startled into reflection. I have no guarantee that these grandchildren of mine will be Christian. Yet, it is my duty to witness to them, or they may not have the opportunity for the choice.

Dr. George Sweazy, who has written so helpfully on evangelism, once said rather effectively that Christianity always faced two challenges: the cemetery and the maternity ward. The former removes the committed saints and does not replace them. The latter welcomes a new generation that does not bring with it an inherited Christian faith. Perhaps God is wise in making it necessary for each man to be responsible for his neighbor, and for each generation to be responsible for the next.

Today the maternity ward has become a real challenge. While the rate of church membership grows by 20-25,000 per day, the population of the world grows ten times that fast. There are now two billion people on the planet who have not heard the Gospel of Jesus Christ. And yet, we must be grateful for the fact that through various means, a knowledge of Jesus is abroad in the earth beyond the confines of the Christian churches. Most school children in Japan know who Jesus is. The influence of Jesus was never greater in the world than it is today, said the late historian, Kenneth Latourette of Yale University. Even so, such general knowledge is hardly sufficient to make disciples of Jesus Christ unless the apostolic mandate is fulfilled personally. Discipleship is more than simply hearing about Jesus of Nazareth; it involves an understanding of his Lordship and an understanding of what commitment to him means in terms of enlistment and education and service.

Crucial Experience

Perhaps the most important aspect of the concept of the Great Commission is its objective. What does it mean to "disciple" a person? That is, what is involved in the process of proclaiming, presenting or announcing the Lordship of Jesus Christ to another person in such a way that he understands and considers the claim and decides to accept it freely and gladly, and commit himself through a crucial decision? What does this meeting or encounter involve?

That such an experience or meeting must take place, whether through a traumatic "moment" or through a series of conversion-like "moments" is essential according to the New Testament. How it takes place is determined by many factors.

The apostle Paul had a revolutionary vision on the road to Damascus. Martin Luther grew up in the church of his day, but after a long ordeal in which he found no peace with God, he was given a new outlook upon life by an awareness of the gospel of grace. John Wesley was in the service of the Church of England, and a missionary in America, before his heart was "strangely warmed" in a chapel on Aldersgate Street, London. And others have gone through less dramatic experiences all through life, passing from one "conversion-like" experience after another in the pilgrimage of their discipleship. A study of the psychology of conversion based upon cases reveals a variety of conversion experiences. A study of the New Testament gives us no one model of discipleship.

Conversion is not alien to the human enterprise. In a sense, man passes through conversions as he moves from one stage of life to another: childhood, adolescence, early adulthood, middle life, agedness. On another level, people are converted to many things, from one tooth paste to another, from one vocation to another, from one religion to another. A change in life is possible when an incentive is strong enough to alter attitudes and focus interest in a new integration and direction.

However, the kind of conversion involved in Christian discipleship is profound and affects the basic direction and purpose of life. To accept the Lordship of Jesus Christ and all that it means is a crucial decision. It involves the ultimate meaning and destiny of life. There is no meeting like this meeting. It is life-cleaving. It is destiny-determining. It goes beyond the mere acceptance of doctrines, or the pledge to reform, or the willingness to join an institution. It is more than an affirmation of a creed. It is the surrender of one's life, the betting of one's existence, the enlistment of one's career. This is an experience that is lonely indeed. Luther spoke of it as being as lonely as dying. Indeed, it is as lonely as being born into life. The apostle Paul said as much when he maintained that he who is "in Christ" is a "new creation" altogether; the old is finished and gone; all has become new.

In the New Testament it is an experience that is compared to dying and rising again. The Christian is one who has been crucified with Christ, and is raised with him to newness of life. Being "in Christ" involves three definite implications: (1) To be in Christ Jesus is to be in him through a personal relationship of faith and obedience; (2) to be in Christ is also to be in his body which is the church; and (3) to be in Christ is to be in his humanity. A disciple is related to Jesus Christ, to his church, and to his mission in and for humanity. The ramifications of the "in Christ" life are as deep and wide and high as the purpose of God in Jesus Christ is for all mankind. It is intimately personal and broadly socio-human.

To be "in Christ" is to be in the Savior from sin, in the Prophet of truth, in the King of righteousness, and in the Servant Lord who came "not to be ministered unto but to minister and give his life a ransom for many." It is to be involved not only in soul, but in body and mind and spirit. It involves the intelligence, affections, and will of the whole human being, for conversion is more than assent to doctrinal propositions, more than emotional response to a moving evangelist's plea, more than an act of response through the exercise of will. To be sure, persons are differently constituted, and some incline more towards one of these aspects than others, but conversion in the Christian sense involves these three to a more or less degree. The Christian is to be a committed, intelligent, and responsible disciple.

Such a conversion is away from an "old" life and its values to the "new" life and its values. It is at once an escape and an adventure. It is both a negative and a positive act: repentance is self-condemnation of the "old" life that is rejected; faith is self-commitment to the "new" life that is offered.

This kind of conversion takes place in the core or marrow of human personality. It does not destroy the self, but it does bring about a change that can be compared only to death and resurrection, burial and revivification. The apostle Paul put it this way, "I live, yet it is no longer I that live, but Christ that lives in me." There is continuity with the old self, but there is also a new creation which is not the product of man's effort or ingenuity; it is the gift and creation of the Spirit of God.

This profound activity brings about the new birth, and starts the self on the road to reconstruction. The process is never completed or perfected; being a disciple of Jesus Christ is a perennial "dying of the old man" and the "putting on of the new man in Christ." The guilt of sin may be forgiven, and the power of sin may be broken, but the "sanctification" or whole-making process goes on until life's end. Conversion cannot be pinned down to a moment; it is a long-term process.

It must be emphasized that this kind of conversion is not self-generated; it always has its initiative in God-in-Christ. It arises from a call to participate in what Christ has done and is doing in the world. It is never a lonely experience; always it is through and in relationships; it is covenantal. It is always pointed towards obedience in the secular world. There is no one accepted model of conversion prescribed for everyone. It is a conversion to the Lord Jesus Christ as the inauguration of the new age, and to the Lord Jesus Christ as the "end" of the age and the consummator of history. It is a call to hope.

There are many definitions of the meaning of the apostolic
ministry. Some have said that it is the task of making Jesus
Christ known, understood, loved and obeyed. D. T. Niles of
Ceylon said it is like one beggar telling another where to get
food. A generation ago it was regarded as a rescue operation to
save souls from the punishment of hell. No one should die without
Christ. Then came others who maintained that it was helping
people to find life in Christ; for it was intolerable to stand
by and see people living without Christ the Life-giver. The
existentialist uses the gospel in order to do something about
himself, to decide about the gospel message for the sake of
bringing unity and integration into the chaos of an absurd human existence. More advanced theologians are saying that God
intends to save the whole world. The locus of God's action is in
the world of nature and present struggles of man for freedom
from hunger, injustice, and everything that dehumanizes him.
The apostle is to broadcast the good news that God has set on
foot a liberating movement which is now in progress, and to
urge men to join in God's enterprise.

Even though we may not agree with some of these concepts of
obedience to the Great Commission, there are several things they
have in common: they believe that something is on foot in history; that it was set in motion by Jesus Christ; that it presents
a claim upon every man's life; that it is a serious matter; that
it does something crucial in the lives of those who accept it;
that it is present now and available; and that it holds the clue
to the meaning of life and history and human destiny.

If this be so, then rethinking the Great Commission will involve a more serious reconsideration of the crucial experience
involved in the disciple-making process that is now the case in
much of our Christianity.

However, we are encouraged by the renewal which is taking
place in many congregations in various parts of the world. One
in particular may be mentioned, since its renewal process is set
within the context of conversion. I refer to the renewal described in *New Life in the Church,* by Robert Raines (Harper).
The chapter headings clearly indicate the process of the project:
the necessity of conversion; conversion begins in awakening;
conversion continues by decision; conversion matures by growth;
conversion endures in discipline; conversion takes place in
Koinonia, the imperative: conversion within the church. Here
is a congregation that takes the Great Commission seriously by
stressing discipleship in its larger context. Other congregations
and Christian groups may pursue somewhat different patterns
of renewal. Whichever the pattern or model, the crucial issue

is whether they keep the major objective of the New Testament in view: the making of the disciple, the new man in Jesus Christ in all his potential manhood or womanhood which conversion to the gospel creates.

Biblical Motif

The apostolic mandate does not rest upon the Great Commission alone. In fact, it is the heart of the biblical message. The Commission crystalizes what is implied in the Scriptures from beginning to end.

The apostolic mandate issues from the good news of the unprecedented action of God centering in Jesus Christ in and through which he inaugurated a new era in history. By it he made all things "new." No wonder the New Testament is such a joyous book, for it announces God-in-action doing something which man could not do for himself.

The apostolic mandate announces that God has visited us; has assumed full responsibility for us; has indentified himself with us so that nothing can separate us from his love; has borne our tragic lot and terrible perversity; has tasted our despair and death; has won a decisive victory of the powers of evil; has opened up "heavenly possibilities" through the resurrection and the power of the Spirit.

The apostolic mandate testifies to the fact that the God in whom we live and move and have our being, who is hidden from our sinful eyes, has revealed himself as Agape (love) ; that he is our torment and our happiness; that he is always at work in history and in life, seeking to correct our disobedience and turn us to himself; that he is the Judge and Ruler and Savior of all nations and peoples who will never find their peace except in willing obedience to the living God; that our personal and social restlessness is but the prodding of God who will give us no rest until we "rest" in his peace (Shalom).

The apostolic mandate proclaims Jesus Christ as the pattern of life, the bearer of sin, the victor over evil powers, the mediator of forgiving mercy, the bearer and Lord of life, the center of fellowship in the church, the inaugurator of God's redemptive activity in history, and the goal of history. Since all power has been given to him, evangelism calls all men to submit their powers to his ultimate power; to make their peace with him.

The apostolic mandate rests upon the "inwardness" and the compulsion of the Pentecostal experience by which the Jesus of history became the indwelling Christ of faith. The same power that raised Christ from the dead raises those "in Christ" to new life, personal and communal. This is no mere "religious" ex-

perience. Paul had a profound sense of being "in Christ" but
he never preached *himself*. The gospel, to Paul, was more a
gift-to-share than a possession-to-claim.

The apostolic mandate is neighbor-love in action offering the
neighbor the greatest gift that God can give. Forgiven sinners
are their brothers' keepers. Christians are free men, yet servants
of all men. The highest service one can render his neighbors is
to invite them to accept and appropriate the gospel.

The apostolic mandate is integral to the nature of the church.
God wills to bring all things together in Christ (Eph. 1). He
wills reconciliation and unity. He wills that all our human relationships be saved and mankind remade into the true family
God intends it to be. Evangelism is the task of inviting persons
to be reconciled to God, and to their fellows. "Christ loved the
church and gave himself up for her" means that the church is
the maternity ward and family and school of God's people whose
mission is to serve God's global purpose. Its task is the celebration, proclamation, demonstration and implementation of God's
gospel-reality.

The apostolic mandate is rooted in the fact of man's lostness
from himself, his neighbor, his work, and his God. Man is "out
of true" "off the beam" of his true nature. His life is not real;
it is a pseudo existence. He tries all sorts of devices to save
himself: alcohol, suicide, sex, drugs, collectivisms, self-worship,
isms of one kind or another. But no man becomes fully man until
he is a Christian; conversion and obedience to Christ start a
man on the way to real humanness.

The biblical bases and theological foundations of evangelism
are deeply rooted in the nature of God-Creator, Redeemer,
Sanctifier. They set man in high perspective and make God's
redemptive action on his behalf something tremendous. The salvation of the world is the immense context in which evangelism
must be seen. Evangelism in this light is no small business for
timid people. Someone has called it "the greatest work in the
world."

It is doubtful whether the Great Commission will be imple-
mented by the Christian or the church unless there is a fresh
revelation of the grandeur and the glory of the Lordship of
Jesus Christ and the gospel he was and brought into life and
history.

All of the human panaceas now offered to remake life and
history lack the one thing needful: they do not have the power
to invite men and women into that context of greatness and
dignity which loyalty to Jesus Christ gives. For life is enhanced

only by that to which it gives itself with heart, soul, mind and strength. With Paul we conclude, "For me to live, is Christ!"

III
RETHINKING THE GREAT COMMISSION

CONDUCT

There are implications in the Great Commission for the conduct of its mandate. The words themselves are compelling: Go! Disciple! Teach! They are a call to action! But these words do not stand by themselves; they are like the conclusion of a mathematical problem. They are the commanding climax of a unique ministry for God and man.

Behind this trumpet-like mandate is the long story of God's revelation-action through Israel which culminated in the Christ-Event in all its fullness. No wonder the Commission breaks in upon the world with a triumphant—Therefore! All that has gone on before is prelude. Now, the march of the gospel may begin down the centuries of time and across the world. The foundation is laid, the formula is completed, the beginning is inaugurated. Now is the time to go, disciple, teach!

And the dimensions of the Commission are staggering. First, its authority is in the sweeping Lordship of Jesus Christ. Second, its scope is the global world of nations. Third, its objective is the enlisting and maturing and equipping of new men in and for Jesus Christ and his cause. Fourth, its goal is the "end" of time. And fifth, its comfort and hope are in the continuing Presence of Jesus Christ in those who engage in the enterprise, and in the humanity into which he was incarnate, for which he died, and in which he lives and acts by his redemptive power.

Much discussion is taking place currently about the conduct of the Great Commission. Old methods are critically examined and in some cases abandoned. New methods are being explored. In face of the new situation confronted by the churches and by Christians the question has been raised afresh: How shall obedience to the Commission be expressed in ways that will preserve the integrity of its content and make relevant and effective the reality of its claim?

Biblical

The conduct of apostleship has much to learn from the method by which the gospel came to us. God is the evangelist, and the good news or the gospel is the report of his breakthrough to man. His truth and love and righteousness have come into life and are made available for human renewal and fulfillment.

It is therefore impossible to think of the gospel as only a
verbal message to be proclaimed through words, although words
are essential in human relations; rather, the gospel includes the
method by which God incarnates himself. God does not speak
one way and act another. Word and deed are one. The very
nature of the gospel as incarnational action links message and
method. The gospel is God's love-in-action.

The Word became flesh and "dwelt" among us. The Incarnation with its wonderful accounts of the birth of Jesus in a lonely
place to humble people in ordinary human circumstances is God's
method of reaching us. Not through a miraculous emergence of
a full-grown hero-god from the head of Zeus, nor through a
fantastic fanfare of royal pomp and circumstance does God come
to us. "The hopes and fears of all the years are met" in a little
town of Bethlehem. This is the way the Word became flesh.

And he dwelt among us in all humanity, humility and servitude. He spoke truth simply and with an inner authority. He
radiated a genuine integrity of grace and truth that attracted
those who were most deeply human. He knew family life. He
worked with his hands. He associated with the sick, the aged,
the children, the ostracized, as well as the rich, the powerful,
the learned, the devout. "He came not to be ministered unto,
but to minister, and give his life as a ransom for many."

The gospel is not primarily a set of theological affirmations,
a list of ethical rules, nor a religious institution. It is God-in-
action in life and history; as such, it has a method all its own.
A careful study of the Gospels will yield a wealth of instruction
on how the Word became flesh in and through Jesus as he
associated with and encountered persons and groups.

Perhaps the first lesson in the conduct of apostolic obedience
to the Great Commission is to realize that the Gospel of the
Lord Jesus Christ is more than a verbal telling of a story;
rather, it is the communication of an unprecedented action of
God in life and history. To be true to his commission, the apostle
must be more than a herald of words; he must be an ambassador
who represents a holy commonwealth as a loyal citizen. He must
first be a disciple who has learned from the Great Evangelist
how to conduct himself in bringing the gospel to all nations.

Incarnational

Much is being written these days about the Incarnation, or
the "infleshing" or the "humanity" of God. It has its application
to the conduct of the apostle who is obedient to the Great Commission. To make disciples and teach is more than telling the

old, old story, significant and precious as it is. The Christian vocabulary has been worn rather thin because it has become so familiar to those inside and outside the churches. And what is more, the distance between the words and the actual lives of Christians has become so great that the words have lost their credibility and their power. The "credibility gap" between the Christian establishment and the realities of the Christian faith have made the Christian verbal witness rather impotent.

Incarnational apostolicity will involve several factors if it is to regain its persuasive power.

First, the apostle will have to identify himself with the situation in which he is to witness. This requires an incarnational self-emptying of anything that would separate him from the people with whom he is to share the Gospel. Any expression of superiority by which he condescends in relating himself to people is a denial of the incarnational principle. Jesus identified himself with humanity in his baptism, even though he had no sins of his own. He was "wedded" to humanity by an indissoluble unity.

Second, incarnational apostolicity engages in an active sharing of life. It involves a participation in the problems and pressures, the fears and frustrations of humanity. It does not approach people with ready-made answers to life's problems; rather, it listens to the questions which people raise.

Third, incarnational apostolicity uses the language and thought forms of the people to whom it brings the gospel. It starts the dialogue. It does not use God-talk, but, like Jesus, uses the language and symbols which people understand. Jesus' language was set in the soil, in the family, and in the carpenter shop. He seldom used religious language. And most of his teaching arose out of life situations.

Fourth, incarnational apostolicity does not bring God *into* the situation. Nor does it convert people *out* of the human situation. Rather, it seeks to make the reality that is in Jesus Christ and the new life he creates through accepting faith, real *in* the human situation.

Fifth, incarnational apostolicity runs the risk of failure. It does not apply force to win a decision. It does not rob the person addressed of his freedom, nor does it interfere with the freedom of the Word and Spirit of God. Jesus applied this principle when he lost the rich young ruler who could not bring himself to accept Jesus' challenge to discipleship.

Conversion is not removing people from their human situation to a sacred place. Nor is it a conversion from the world God created. Rather, it is making known the presence of God in

Jesus Christ in the world where men live so they may have new life in him *where they are.*

Incarnational apostolicity goes *to* the nations; it speaks the language of different peoples; it makes disciples of Jesus Christ in their local cultures; it breaks out of traditional language and forms to make the Incarnate Christ known who has infilled the whole body of humanity with his continuing presence, power and prospect.

Natural

The Commission was given to the original disciples. They were no extraordinary men. Perhaps only one was equipped with unusual gifts: John. They represented a cross-section of the rank and file of humanity. Yet, to them, and to all Christians who succeed them in history, was given the staggering task of communicating the gospel, enlisting nationals of the entire globe in discipleship, and of educating them into mature and responsible men and women under the Lordship of Jesus Christ. They are the new body of humanity in and through which Christ would reach all men and penetrate their society by what was in him.

This is at once an impossible assignment and a glorious privilege. Who is able to fulfill that Commission! And yet, it was to ordinary people that the Commission was directed. The apostle Paul put it this way to the Corinthian Christians, "God did beseech you by *us.*" There is no other way. Many people have the idea that the communication of the gospel must be done in extraordinary and spectacular ways. But God honors ordinary means of communication and everyday human relationships. There is no divine esperanto or Kingdom-talk which possesses magical powers of persuasion. There will be "no angel visitant, no opening skies, no sudden rending of this veil of clay" to communicate the gospel. This task will be done through human beings and human means, even as it was done in and through the man, Jesus Christ.

While this is an impossible assignment, it is also a glorious privilege. God honors ordinary people, human language, personal relationships, and local situations. He provides us an opportunity to share in the ministry of bringing the good news to the neighbor. In so doing, we partake in the very work of God in remaking persons and fulfilling God's purpose. Little wonder that the apostle Paul rejoiced in his ambassadorship for Christ and to the world. As an ambassador, he had the royal and dignified task of representing his Kingdom-nation, commending its qualities to other nations and cultures, and of making peace. Such a vocation demands expert diplomacy on the part of the ambassador!

God has entrusted this high responsibility and privilege to us humans. We are our brother's keepers; we are responsible for each other. We are invited to share in God's grand and gracious purpose for all mankind!

Ethical

The conduct of apostleship must be done in conformity with the nature of the gospel. The end never justifies the means in communicating the gospel.

Even Jesus was tempted at this point. After his baptism into his vocation for God and man, he was "driven" into the wilderness to be tested. The temptations have several meanings, one of which has to do with methods of winning disciples.

The first temptation was to prostitute his ministry to man's desire for bodily and physical satisfactions. Give men bread—and cake—and they will follow you! But Jesus rejected this method. It interpreted the total need of man as a craving for physical welfare only. It made God into a redeemer of the body only. To Jesus, bread was so important that he included it in his model prayer; it was a gift of God for man's need. But it must not be elevated into man's *one* great need.

The second temptation was an appeal to use political and military force to bring the world to submission. This temptation was rejected for it made the supreme good an ordered society shaped by freedom-denying coercion, and it reduced God to mass power.

The third temptation was to attract people by performing a spectacular stunt. Again, Jesus refused to make God and his Kingdom an object of entertainment. Such a method may attract crowds who stand agape at the sight, but it does not enlist persons in obedient discipleship to Christ's cause. The Kingdom of God is of utmost interest to man, but it is not a circus.

The apostle Paul puts it graphically in his second Letter to the Corinthians, according to J. B. Phillips' translation: "We use no hocus-pocus, no clever tricks, no dishonest manipulation of the Word of God. We speak the plain truth . . . For it is Christ Jesus the Lord whom we preach not ourselves; we are your servants, for His sake." (II Cor. 4)

The gospel must not be distorted or falsified by unusual methods of communication. The earthen vessels through which it is proclaimed undoubtedly shape the form of the gospel, but they must not enhance themselves at the expense of the gospel's content.

Communal

Obedience to the Great Commission involves a corporate witness of Christ's disciples. It is impossible to think of Jesus apart from his disciples. From the beginning of his ministry, he was associated with the twelve whom he regarded as the nucleus of the New Israel he came to inaugurate. Jesus never thought of himself as a personal guru or religious leader interested only in stimulating individuals to cultivate a personal piety. He regarded himself as the fulfiller of Israel, the source of a new Kingdom-age, and the center of the New Covenant—people of God. In short, Jesus Christ set into motion a new life and a new community. Both are called to an apostolic ministry committed to make him known, loved and obeyed among all nations.

One of the most effective ways in which Christians fulfilled with apostolic witness in the early Christian centuries was through their community life, whether in families or congregations. Life in the community was a compelling witness to a world that knew little of the truth and love and righteousness of the Christian community. Congregations were oases of personal support and bases of mission. The world took note that Christians loved one another, and that they were concerned for the poor and unfortunates who were victims of an unjust society. The sheer power of their corporate witness even in persecution wielded a powerful influence in that old and hard world.

The gospel is communicated corporately. Christianity is a community faith. Indeed, the gospel is social from beginning to end. The gospel is aimed to create a new humanity. This social witness is integral to the apostolic obedience.

We must confess that our churches for the most part are aggregations of individuals and not fellowships of the Spirit. They are often closed societies of people drawn from the world, who immure themselves in self-protective walls, and preserve themselves from the world. Such churches are no longer pattern communities, common fellowships, mission societies.

Every congregation should strive not only to conserve its heritage and its tradition, but to extend its fellowship into the community. Each congregation should seek to realize the democracy of the Spirit, the real home and family of God, which by its very nature is seeking to win all men to fellowship in its life. The late Dr. Temple once said in effect that the Church of England trained its ministers to conserve the faith of the Church, but it did not train them to be aggressive conquerors of the world of Christ. Little wonder, then, that enthusiastic sects and cults have arisen to provide people with a sense of belonging to something that has warmth and brotherly love; that cell groups are growing up outside the churches to provide the lonely with a fellowship that stimulates and encourages; that one of the greatest challenges to the world Church today is a movement that has perverted the lovely term Communion into "Communism."

No wonder the World Council of Churches at its New Delhi assembly recommended a continuation of the study on the missionary structure of the local congregation. If the congregation is God's mission-in-action, then perhaps many of its structures need to be examined and changed if it is to fulfill its apostolic purpose. Too many churches are self-centered; they make it their primary purpose to preserve themselves from the world. And too many churches are more interested in preserving their past traditions when the Great Commission of the church's Lord bids them to go into all the world. To be church, it is not enough to preach the Word of God faithfully, administer the Sacraments, exercise administrative order and discipline; to these "marks" of the church must be added that of being true to the apostolic mandate! This concept of church renewal makes quite a difference in the nature and conduct of worship, in preaching, in education, in pastoral care, in social service and action, and in ecumenical outreach.

This corporate apostolate expresses itself in many forms. One of its most potent forms is the Christian family, the primary group in which the nature of God's love, truth and righteousness finds its finest expression. Since the Christian faith is set in a family context, the churches should regard the family as its best ally in communicating and implementing the gospel in the common life.

Another form is that of the small group meeting informally, whether inside or outside church buildings. In them, open dialogue regarding many matters of life and faith may be discussed in freedom. Within the past few decades such groups have arisen in Europe and America in the form of house churches, worker-priests, academies, coffee houses, disciplined communities like Iona and Taize, and inner-city "store front" communities. They have all been part of a search for the renewal of the early Christian community.

The question may be asked, "What is first—the verbal proclamation of the gospel, or the communal expression and presence of the gospel?" *Both* are essential to a full communication of the gospel. However, since the Christian faith is communal in nature, the fulfillment of the apostolic witness is incomplete without the "presence" of that Christian fellowship which creates the climate of acceptance and confidence in which the gospel is best heard and experienced. This truth has been expressed in the ministry of counseling. Pre-counseling is not counseling itself, but before anyone will seek out the church counselor, a prior cultivation of friendship must be established. Words are not enough, nor should they be separated from the group. Through community and interpersonal relationships, words become effective.

What about the mass meeting? Since Christianity is a communal faith, there is a place for the social celebration of the gospel through sermon, song and prayer. It not only strengthens the faith of those already committed to Jesus Christ, but sets the gospel in the life of the community. Such a public celebration is best conducted in unity and in harmony with the nature and purpose of the gospel. In a day of ecumenical relations, it may well include Roman Catholics, Protestants, and Orthodox, and other interested Christians. Such a social witness would have a powerful effect upon the world!

Personal

Every Christian has an apostolic commission. The very nature of the new life in Christ is dynamically compulsive. With the apostle Paul, the Christian exclaims: "Woe is me if I preach not the gospel!" Such a boon cannot be "hid under a bushel" or kept under wraps. It is meaningful discovery that wants to be shared with every man. To quote Paul again, in his great defense before a Roman court, "Would that all men were like me, except these bonds." (Acts 26)

In spite of the fact that relations have grown more impersonal, and individuals are absorbed increasingly into large organizations, the power of personal influence is *still* immeasurable. Indeed, it may be more so than in the past. Who can estimate the influence of a Christian parent on his children? Or the personal influence of a teacher on students? Or the effect of a pastor upon a congregation or a community? Or that of a national leader on people of a country, or of the world?

Every individual has a sphere of influence. It is at once a gift of God and a power over which responsibility is to be exercised. It can be used for good or for ill. Jesus passed a severe condemnation on anyone who would offend "one of the least of these." The apostle Paul believed that the life of a believing Christian wife might have power to win the non-Christian partner to discipleship for Christ.

The Christian layman is called upon to exercise his apostolic ministry. Protestants and Roman Catholics are united in their emphasis upon apostolate of the laity. Laymen have been called the "frozen assets" of the Christian community. They are the church, not only when they are in the sanctuary, classroom, or social hall of a church building. Through baptism, the layman is ordained into the life and service of Jesus Christ. A layman's ministry is not primarily or only that of helping the ordained, or set-apart, minister of the church to "run" the church; rather, the ordained minister is to equip the layman to fulfill his ministry as a servant of Christ in the world. And that means to make his witness felt in his family, his profession, his community. This is the way the gospel of the Lordship of Jesus Christ makes its witness felt in suburbia, in the inner city, in the college and university, in centers of power, and in the fields of leisure, mass media, industry, and education.

The apostolate of the laity, if taken seriously, would bring about many changes in churches. It would certainly change the clergy-role from that of administrator-director of an institution to that of pastor-teacher-leader of the people of God. It would give worship a fresh meaning. It would give clearer direction to Christian education. It would give the whole church a purpose more oriented towards the life and work of the layman in the world. And the power of the gospel, while still generated and fostered in the gathered Christian community would become a force in the secular community. After all, Christians are the light and salt of the earth; as such, their main function is *in* the world.

The layman can penetrate the world as the minister cannot. He speaks the language of his craft or profession. He brings the witness into the secular relationships of life. He lives and works on the frontier where the kingdom of God and the kingdom of this world meet in dialogue and encounter. He is the "presence" and the witness of the gospel in the secular world.

Theological education is related to the apostolate of the laity. Theological education not only acquaints prospective ministers of churches with the fascinating lore of the Christian faith, helps them to think theologically, forms them as men of God, and trains them in the essential skills of Christian leadership; it is also responsible for educating leaders who can mature and equip the lay apostolate for their ministry in the world.

Verbal

The gospel is communicated verbally and vocally. How shall men "hear" without a "preacher," and how shall they preach unless they have experienced something compelling? The power of speech when fired by an experience becomes a potent witness.

It is one of God's finest gifts to us humans. By it we communicate with one another. And the preacher who makes a public witness not only arrests his hearers; his witness penetrates into the very marrow of their spirits.

Protestantism has always believed in preaching, but it has not always warned sufficiently against clever preaching which deprives God of His glory and the hearer of his freedom. However, the witness of a preacher who preaches the living Word for the church, to the church and through the church, is still one of the finest means of communicating the gospel to the community. Only, let him preach the gospel and not himself. Let him preach simply to the deep hungers of the human spirit, in the language of the newspaper if need be, but with a view to winning a verdict. Let him preach with clear intention and not merely for the sake of discussing an interesting theme. Many a preacher had better inquire about his *intention* in preaching and not worry so much about his sermon *themes!* All preaching of the Word should lead to worship, to a re-commitment to discipleship, to the great decision to either believe the gospel, or to turn away from it. Let there be no moratorium on real gospel preaching; but let the preacher remember that he is preaching the gospel for the nurture and apostleship of the church.

But the gift of speech is not confined to the trained preacher. The whole church is to witness to the gospel. And the whole church means every member of it. Laymen are to be witnesses not only in their church school teaching, but in their homes, in their places of work, and in their life-situations. The layman's voice can reach more people and places than that of the minister. The layman uses the gift of speech for a thousand things, but he seldom uses it to speak about the glory of the God who gave it! We may be thankful to God for the revival in our time of the lay apostolate. The tongue of the whole church is to be unloosed.

This vocal witness needs to be extended to the radio and to television. We have not yet learned how to speak the convincing Word to the radio and TV listener. Some persons have the gift; but even so, radio and TV are too remote from the listener to bring about a real encounter and decision. While these modern means of communication have great potentialities, they have not as yet been used to their full potential and with enough strategic study to serve the gospel effectively along evangelistic lines.

We are in a communications revolution. The form as well as the extent of communication is making it possible to reach the peoples of the entire earth with the Christian message. Seeing and hearing will be combined in a dramatic way. The word and the life will be linked as it is in the gospel and as it is in the new life in Christ. This atomic explosion in communications must be put at the service of Jesus Christ in a new burst of apostolic thrust.

Hopeful

Perhaps the greatest need in fulfilling the apostolic mandate is motivation. The apostolic task depends upon the apostolic spirit of the apostle. He must know what it means to be "sent" by a compelling authority or experience. Without this he suffers a loss of nerve and loses his apostolic motivation.

The strongest motivation, of course, is in Jesus Christ. James Denney once heard a distinguished missionary say that the people who do not believe in missions are not Christians; they do not believe in Jesus Christ. New Testament Christians took the gospel everywhere because they believed that Jesus Christ was Lord; that he had ultimate authority in heaven and in earth. They believed he was Lord of nations, that his spirit was at work in history, and that his ministry would be consummated at the end of the age. They did not *make* him Lord and King. Every page of the New Testament affirms that in him the kingdom of God has broken into history, a new beginning has been made in life, and that a process has been let loose which will one day be consummated. They were constrained to make the event known and to invite people to enter this secret of life and history.

These early apostles believed this Lordship of Jesus Christ was to be extended to include all nations. It was an enterprise that was global and ecumenical in its sweep. It was not confined to the disciples, nor to the Jews, nor to Palestine. It had a grand and glorious character about it. This is what motivated them in spite of their frailties and weaknesses. They believed this action of God in Jesus Christ was crucial in the life of man and nations. It was news of an unprecedented action. They believed that what Jesus Christ started would continue to the end of the age. They were living and witnessing in the wave of that future. Their apostolic zeal was motivated by that future hope, a hope that was already at work in them and in the world. They learned from Jesus that he did not come to restore the past, but to fulfill it. Their apostolate was future-oriented.

Because of this act of God in Jesus Christ, the apostles believed that human life could be initiated into the new possibilities which Jesus Christ made available. Life's meaning could be restored and its intention fulfilled. Those who were in Christ were new creations. And they belonged to the community of God's secret; they were the inheritors of the future, the first fruits of God's redemptive action in Christ Jesus. The apostles had no doubt whatever that something could happen to individuals who believed in Jesus Christ. They could become sons and daughters of God through faith and the power of the Holy Spirit. They could be "saved" from a false life to a true life.

Apostolic obedience is motivated by a fresh awareness of the grandeur and the glory of the gospel of Jesus Christ. There is no other motivation!

In Conclusion

Permit me to conclude with a few suggestions on our subject which could each be elaborated into rather lengthy papers. First, evangelism must be done *relevantly*. The gospel must be aimed at the critical issues which men face today. This does not mean that we shall adapt the gospel to what men think they want; rather, we shall interpret the gospel so that the agitations of men's spirits may be seen in their true light. Men want "peace of mind," but it is not our task to give them an easy peace on their own terms. The gospel gives peace, indeed, but it gives a peace according to God's will and grace. In our parish ministries, we ought to be sensitive to the crises of individuals and families and groups, so as to be on hand when trouble strikes.

The communication of the gospel today must be done *identifyingly;* that is, in the spirit of love for those to whom we would minister. I am often amazed at the humanity of our Lord. There was nothing of the snob about him. Though he was rich, for our sakes he became poor; he took upon himself the form of a servant; he identified himself with us in all points. His "point of contact" with men was in his common humanity. In conversing with the woman at the well of Samaria, he did not start with theological doctrine; he started with the request for a drink of water! All through his ministry, he started where people were. Evangelism cannot be done in the spirit of pride or of pity for the "heathen." We are discovering this truth in our relations with Christians in the younger churches. Perhaps the church will have to become great enough in our time to become human!

The communication of the gospel must be done *prayerfully*. Evangelism at its best is intercessory prayer in action. We never care about others until we make them the object of our intercession with God. Prayer opens doors into the hearts of others and it releases the power of the Spirit. It acknowledges the place of humility in fulfilling the apostolic commission. And it confesses that only the power of the Holy Spirit can make the apostle's witness understood and create the miracle of appropriating faith.

The apostolic task must be done *expectantly*, that is, in the full confidence that Jesus Christ can change life. The gospel has the power to transform life. The gospel can produce a "happening" in persons! Perhaps we have handled the Word of Life so much that it has lost its novelty and its power. The spirit of spontaneity has gone from much of our Christian life and church work. We carry on our ecclesiastical "business as usual," little realizing that the gospel can make a world of difference in men's lives. Think of Jesus and his conversation with the woman at the Samaritan well. The situation was impossible. Yet, he led her from a drink of water on up to the satisfying living water. To her, he disclosed some of the greatest truths ever revealed to man. Had Jesus gone by our human categories, he would have written the whole conversation off as a waste of time. Little wonder that he declared that the harvest of men's spirits was ripe for ingathering. Wait four months? Make a lot of preparation? Put it off until the times are more propitious? No, says our Lord, opportunities are awaiting us every day, in the most unlikely Samarias, and at the most inappropriate times. If such a thing could happen to such a woman in such a situation, what may happen anywhere, anytime, to anybody? Evangelism may be done seasonally and after some careful preparation; it ought to be done always and everywhere. Jesus Christ impregnates every "secular" situation with "eternal" possibilities. But before anything can happen, we will have to believe that it can happen, that men do seek God, that every moment is potentially sacramental with the divine presence and power.

2

The Language Problem in Evangelism

by JAMES D. SMART

Evangelism has a language problem. The "evangel" is simply the gospel, the word of truth of Jesus, the Christ spoken by Jesus and lived out by him in his life and death that opens doors between God and man and thereby transforms the character and meaning of life. That word of truth may be communicated in many different ways. The one thing that matters is that, whatever form of communication it finds, it be with integrity the word of truth that has its origin in the Jesus of the Scriptures. It can find its way from person to person in a chance remark in conversation, in a theological lecture, in the singing of a hymn, in the offering of a prayer, in a public protest against injustice, and of course in a sermon, which has the uniqueness of being a deliberate and responsible public attempt to speak that word of truth. Moreover the sermon does not have to have some one particular form to be the "evangel." All that is necessary is that somewhere, somehow in it the word of truth which is a doorway to newness of life makes itself heard. But now the problem: unfortunately, the words "evangel" and "evangelism" do not have that breadth of scope in the minds of most church members. Their significance is narrowed. The words conjure up primarily a mass-meeting presided over by an "evangelist" who is an expert at securing instant conversions.

It is not difficult to show that Jesus in no way conforms to the pattern of the modern "evangelist." It is true that at times there were large crowds which gathered to hear him but there is no indication either that he was a spell-binder as a speaker, or that he had a method of eliciting immediate decisions, or, for that matter, that he had much success in persuading the crowds to accept his gospel. He seems to have been content, like the prophets before him, to let his message be heard, with all its sharp

James D. Smart is Professor of Biblical Interpretation, Union Theological Seminary, New York, New York. The article included here is one of a series of *Occasional Papers on Evangelism* published by the Division of Evangelism of The United Presbyterian Church in the U.S.A. It is used here by permission.

edges showing, and to leave it to bear its harvest in God's own good time. At the close of his mission in Galilee, not many days before his death, he had only a handful of converts to show for all his efforts. It hardly needs to be pointed out that all the appurtenances of modern evangelism are absent—the careful advance promotion, the massed choirs, the whole musical and psychological build-up, the professional encouragers, the follow-up campaign. All of these may be quite legitimate in their place, but it is important to recognize that evangelism as it originated with Jesus and his disciples was of a quite different character and that, without discounting the achievements of mass evangelism in the past two centuries, our present need is to take our start afresh from the evangelism of Jesus and rethink its implications for our life as Christians in the world of today.

Our language problem is that two centuries of mass evangelism have fastened on certain key words of the New Testament meanings similar to what has happened to "evangel" "evangelism" and "evangelist." "Conversion" now means to most people a once-in-a-lifetime experience in which a person is transformed from an unbeliever into a believer, although in the Scriptures the power of God's word to judge and redeem makes the hearing of it, if it be truly heard, a constant force of change or conversion in human life, and not just in the individual but in the society of which he is a part. The narrowing of meaning in the word "conversion" constitutes a serious perversion of the biblical perspective and tragic limitation on the scope of the gospel's power.

A parallel example is what has happened to the Johannine term "born again." It has been made a synonym for "conversion" and is usually identified with the experience of anyone who has made a decision at an evangelistic meeting. But in the Gospel of John, it has no such association. In John 1:12, 13, verses point to pre-Christian times when the Word was and persons through the Word had their life in God. A key doctrine of John's Gospel is that the only true life of man is life in God, life in openness to God's judgment and love. A man may be ever so religious and moral and may be quite confident that he believes in God and yet not be open to the Word in which his life is constantly judged and renewed in the presence of God. "Nicodemus in John 3 was such a man, outstanding as a representative of religion and morality, a good man, a man humble in his approach to Jesus, but not yet willing to have himself laid unconditionally open to the sovereign power of God's word. The Word, incarnate, was there before him in Jesus. To receive it, to be open to it, to let it have its way with him, would have meant letting go of the established securities of his present religious position and launching out into an uncharted new future. The Word of God, both in the Old Testament and the New, shakes men loose from the static religious order in which their lives have become embedded and sets them free to be at God's service in his shaping of the future. Therefore, to be born of the Word, born of God, born again, means that, whatever one's life and religion has been before, his hearing of the Word makes him willing to break with all his old loyalties and securities and to begin his life afresh in openness and obedience to whatever that Word may want to make of him. How strange it is then that so many Christians who claim to have been "born again" seem to have been made intensely conservative by the experience, anchored to forms of religion, theology and practice that belong more to the past than to the present, and open only to a future that conforms to long-established religious patterns! In the first century to be born of the Word and Spirit made Christians revolutionaries who turned the world upside down. How then can 20th century men and women who profess to have been born again be so often the most stubborn opponents of change both in the church and in the social order?

It is clear, then, that we have a language problem in evangelism, a very difficult language problem. A set of meanings has been fastened on words essential to our venture which obscure their original meaning in Scripture, which misrepresent the character of Christian evangelism, and which alienate many of our church members from the whole enterprise. Think only of what has happened to the word "saved," one of the richest and most meaningful words in the Scriptures. The context which it immediately calls up in most of our minds is not biblical at all but consists of three words which we have had addressed to us by various persons at various times in our lives—"Are you saved?" The impression has long been abroad that the only way to participate in personal evangelism is to go about asking people, "Are you saved?" Let it be granted at once that thousands of people have been provoked by that question to serious consideration of their relationship with God and that those who asked the question were at least trying very earnestly to do something about evangelism, in contrast to their Christian brethren who absolve themselves of all responsibility for communicating the gospel to anyone else. But nevertheless it is possible that this use of the word "saved" does more harm than good to the Christian cause. We shall understand why this is so only if we first make clear to ourselves the biblical meaning of the words "save" and "salvation" and then compare the biblical meaning with the meaning implicit in the traditional question.

In the Old Testament God is Israel's Saviour. The nation throughout its life looked back to the deliverance from Egypt as God's great saving act. They were slaves in Egypt with no hope of any future when Moses had revealed to him the care of God for such an afflicted people. It was God's purpose to free them from their bondage to make them a nation in covenant with him, dedicated to his service. In the song of triumph after their deliverance they sang, "The Lord is my strength and my song, and he has become my salvation." (Exodus 15:2) Salvation here is a political event which could have its modern parallel in the liberation of a Negro population from a state of subjection, or the emancipation of a people from the grasp of an exploitive tyranny. The God of Moses was the enemy of exploitation, oppression and tyranny and Moses' commitment of himself to such a God meant that he put himself at his service for the effecting of his revolutionary and transforming purpose. Salvation for Israel was first of all a political deliverance which then issued in a covenant relation with the God who saved them and meant their permanent enlistment in his service.

It is not surprising then that God's saving acts throughout the Old Testament had to do with the deliverance of the nation, when its future was endangered by enemies or by corruption within the nation itself. The prophets insisted century by century that the possibility of a future depended upon the sustaining of the covenant relation with God. Unless the justice, mercy and truth of God was mirrored in the life of Israelites with each other, the nation would not survive. Salvation for Israel depended upon the response of its people to God, not just in some secret place of the soul but in the ordinary every day situations of life. To be right with God meant justice for rich and poor alike, kindness to the helpless and the foreigner and an end to every form of exploitation and oppression. It is this basic biblical understanding of God and of man's covenant relation with God that comes for forceful expression in the Confession of 1967, and particularly in its paragraphs concerning racial discrimination, poverty and war. Reconciliation means oneness with the God of the Scriptures who loves the creatures he has made and hates everything that robs them of their opportunity for the life he has designed for them. To be reconciled with him is to be joined with him in an uncompromising and unending struggle to deliver his children of every race and color from their bondage in a modern Egypt.

A salvation of the "soul" as a transaction of inner "spiritual" life, quite apart from man's every day life in community, is unknown to prophets and psalmists. In fact, the word translated "soul" is better rendered by "self," for it compasses the whole existence of a man in all his relationships. The God of the Scriptures does not limit his interest to so-called "spiritual things" but is concerned with the totality of the world's life. God's love is for the world and the focus of his work of reconciliation is upon the world. The prophets were constantly having to contend with people who thought they could guarantee a right relation with God by acts of worship or the acceptance of correct principles. But what alone interested the prophet, because to him it was the sole interest of God, was whether or not the people in their daily life with each other were open and responsive to God's word of promise and command. A true Israel was an Israel faithful to its commission. So also the Confession of 1967 defines a true church not by the beauty of its worship or the quality of its preaching or the success of its programs but by its obedience to its sending. It has been sent to the world with a ministry of reconciliation and it can justify its existence before God only insofar as it fulfills that ministry. Salvation is the life in covenant with God which no man can possess for himself unless he is willing to let it reach beyond him to the world at his door.

The prophet who uses the word salvation most often is Second Isaiah. He looks backward to the creation and the exodus as God's mightiest acts in the past and then forward to a new creation, a new era in human existence, a new deliverance for Israel and mankind that will make the old exodus be forgotten. God's sovereignty will be established over the whole earth and every knee will bow to him. Salvation for the prophet comprehends the whole creation. The promise of the word which God has spoken in Israel's past is that war, poverty, injustice and the whole chaos created by man's blindness and perversity will one day be overcome and God's love for man prevail in the order of the world's life. In the present hour of darkness and disorder a man survives by trusting that word and, living in openness to God and to his brother, begins already to taste the joy and triumph that are to come. He is saved from futility and despair by holding fast to the word that claims him utterly for God. What Second Isaiah called salvation and could even describe as a new heaven and earth, Jesus called "the kingdom of God" or "the kingdom of heaven." To Jesus the folly of men was that they were blind to God, and those who were most preoccupied with religious concerns, most diligent in their attendance at religious worship, most devoted in their study of the Scriptures and most insistent upon obedience to the law of God were frequently blindest to the present reality of God's intention and purpose. Jesus' mission was not to secure from men decisions to believe in God and be religious. The most stubborn opposition to his mission was from men who believed in God and were intensely religious.

His mission was to open men's eyes to the presence of God with them, to free them from the crippling consequences of their sins with his forgiveness, to take their little empty lives up into the rich unfolding of his redemptive purpose for mankind, and to set them in motion toward the fulfillment of their only true life in God's kingdom. Jesus was not interested in numbers but rather in the shaping of a community of men and women who in their openness to the Spirit and Word of God would be really open to the future that God had in store for them. He turned men away who let themselves be bound to the past in such a way that they were not free for their future. The gospels and the book of Acts show us the obstacles he had to overcome even in his most devoted disciples in order to create that community of God's new age. Their salvation was already present insofar as they were committed to him and to his gospel and were open to what he would make of them; but their salvation both as individuals and as members of a society for which they were responsible had still to come to them insofar as they and the world of which they were a part were still estranged from God and resistant to his rule. Thus while with joy they saw the kingdom already breaking in upon them and setting them free for their life as children of God, they had to pray each day afresh, "Thy kingdom come," and recognize to what a small degree the kingdom had as yet come either in their own lives or in the world about them. The disciples lived in tension between the salvation already accomplished in them through Jesus and his gospel and the salvation that was in store for them and for mankind in the purposes of God. Never were they allowed to become complacent or cocksure in the contemplation of what they had experienced. Their continuing involvement in the sin and blindness of their world, and their consciousness of the distance between what they were and what in the intention of God they were yet to be, were sufficient to keep them humble.

The same picture emerges in the letters of Paul. It is interesting that where Jesus in the first three gospels speaks of the kingdom of God, the Fourth Gospel usually has the term "life" or "eternal life" and Paul speaks of "salvation." But all three terms signify both a present and a future reality. The kingdom is present and yet it is expected and prayed for. The believer "has" eternal life and yet the goal that is set before him is the realization of eternal life. So also with Paul, we are saved from sin and death and from a life of futility by faith through grace, and yet this new life that we already have in Christ is only a foretaste of what God is yet to accomplish in us and through us. It is time now to ask how the contemporary use of the word "saved" and "salvation" tallies with the biblical use. Surely a great gulf yawns between them! The Bible is talking about life, true life, the realization of a relation with God which enables me to be really human, really myself, in all my life's relationships. Salvation is life and has in it the promise of a fulfillment of life beyond all imagining. But what has the questioner in mind who stops me on the street and asks me, "Are you saved?" I can remember a number of such occasions when I took the trouble to find out what my questioner had in mind. Invariably he had a theology in which he divided all humanity into the saved and the damned and he identified the saved as those who had undergone an experience of conversion which he was prepared to define. Usually he was doubtful if anyone could be saved except in the religious group to which he himself belonged. Usually also it was a salvation that guaranteed chiefly one's place in a future heaven, salvation of the soul, rather than the beginning of a reconciling world of God that would have in it the promise of a transformation of the everyday world. Invariably the conversion meant commitment in every particular to the viewpoint and the practices of the community in which the conversion was to occur. Far from being a liberation to be free for God's shaping of the future, it was a binding of the convert, body and soul, to the religious group and its ideology.

We have a language problem indeed. It makes our situation difficult if we are really committed to the mission of Jesus Christ. But a difficult situation is not a hopeless situation if we are willing to deal honestly and intelligently with the problem. The solution is to let our evangelism recover its roots in the Scriptures and to learn from the Scriptures first a way of seeing, and then a way of speaking, that will be in closer correspondence with how God in that earlier day got on most effectively with his work of salvation among men.

Salvation is not a state of soul but a movement in history, an invasion of our blind and broken world by God's new world of grace and truth. There is no salvation for any of us unless we welcome that divine invasion each day afresh, and let ourselves be caught up and carried forward by it into a new future.

3

To Engage in Society With God for Man

by A. DUDLEY WARD

No longer is it tenable for the church to live in its traditional role in response to the universe and its people. If it does, the church will become speedily a non-essential element of a moving, modern world. It is not sufficient any longer for the church simply to respond to what other people do, or what other people feel. The church must initiate, which does not preclude a thorough-going involvement with other persons and institutions.

This role is difficult, but is the theme of the Judaeo-Christian faith in response to the promptings of God and his movement in history. It means, for example, that extremely high importance must be given to the enrichment and nourishment of interior, spiritual, and emotional needs of people and society.

The church must respond to the energetic, almost frantic search of people today for values having reality. The traditional, archaic, outmoded theological forms and jargon that still characterize the Christian church are no longer tenable. They are the source of much of the church's hang-up with the world. Nevertheless, the hippie world, for instance, uses symbols such as the turtle neck, which looks like a clerical collar; a medallion on a chain, which looks very much like what some religious hierarchies wear; beads, which are a favorite symbol in all religions, including Christianity; flowers, which adorn the altar; ponchos that look like the vestments of the clergy. Why is this? When man searches for reality, he looks toward symbols that are well ordered and have continuity with his entire history.

Men search for a social order based upon values that make sense and are cohesive, with objectives that captivate the imagination, stir the energies and motivate the spirit.

A. Dudley Ward is the General Secretary of the Board of Christian Social Concerns of The United Methodist Church. He is the author of Secular Man in Sacred Mission, published by TIDINGS. "To Engage in Society With God for Man" first appeared in engage magazine, published by the Board of Christian Social Concerns of The United Methodist Church. It is used here with permission.

Men search for a social order in which they can devote their creative powers toward building, rather than killing and destroying; toward putting people ahead of money; toward peace instead of military power; toward dealing with crime and violence creatively in terms of its root causes. In this context the church is called to be absolutely honest about its own life and about the assumptions it brings to its mission in the world.

We are faced with a new realism about society in which the church must recognize that the human drama is under the guidance and direction of the God of history, who is telling us something new and distinct about himself and his universe. This new realism will prevent us from becoming upset by patterns, conduct, and mechanisms that have not been used or accommodated in the past by the church. The church has its own special forms of archaic expression and action. Against these it must bring new theological formulations, a new social realism, and new strategies. It must be willing to risk involvement on deeper levels than ever before, without becoming an unreliable judge with pretentions it has no right to assume.

The church must continue to provide positive suggestions, adequate critical analysis, and fundamental understanding of the use of varieties of sound political and spiritual power in a responsible way as attempts are made to deal directly with the essential needs of people. In this, the church must become increasingly accustomed to moving in such situations with humility, grace, and a confidence that is sensitive to the needs and aspirations of leaders and those who follow.

4

The Glory of It All

by IRA GALLOWAY

II Corinthians 4:5-17; 5:17-6:1

"We have this treasure," Paul says, "in earthen vessels." And I want to share some thoughts with you *that we do have the treasure*, and it is in earthen vessels, but also *profoundly* that the vessel remains, in my opinion, *an empty earthen vessel without the treasure*. But, *we have this treasure*, even though in earthen vessels. *That's our glory*, if we have any glory at all.

A look at our world: A couple of years ago I had a graphic look at the world in which we live as a guide took me to a prison in Berlin. This was not the prison where Hitler executed the Jews but where he tortured and killed his most personal enemies. Plotzensee Prison was its name. We walked into a room and there were eight meat-hooks hanging there. The men and women were put up there, eight at a time and stools were kicked out from under them and they hung until they were dead. But in the next room, I saw something that perhaps shocked me more than anything else has ever shocked me in my life, for I walked into a room and came face to face with a guillotine. Hitler saved this for those he despised the most. And some twenty-five short years ago there in Berlin, modern, civilized men and women were being laid on a block with a massive blade being dropped and their heads cut off. The world in which we live! Man come of age?

Dr. Pitirin, the Harvard sociologist, has stated, "Not only war, famine, pestilence and revolution but a legion of other calamities are rampant over the world.

"All values are unsettled," this sociologist says, "all norms are broken. Mental, moral, aesthetic and social anarchy reigns."

C. P. Snow, the renowned British historian, confessed in a speech at Fulton College, "I am nearer to despair this year, 1968, than ever before in my life. Everything points in the

Ira Galloway is superintendent of the Fort Worth East District of The United Methodist Church. He is President of the United Methodist Council on Evangelism. The article included here is a portion of a sermon delivered to the 1969 meeting of the United Methodist Council on Evangelism.

direction of anti-hope. In 1967 you could feel this, this year, you can see it."

I saw this despair very graphically as I flew into Kansas City on a plane. A young woman sat by the window. Jim Patterson, a layman from one of the churches in our community, and I sat in the seats next to her. She had a little baby. We had our meals served and we began to eat. In a conversation with her, she shared that she hadn't eaten in a couple of days. She had to stay overnight at Love Field. And so, we hurriedly finished our eating, cleared our tables and asked if we might take the baby and hold her. As we were holding the baby, to make conversation, I said to her, "Are you going home, or coming from home, or what?" She said, "I'm going home. It's the only place I have to go. My husband was killed last week in Vietnam. And Mama said she would take care of us until we could work it out."

Man, right there—that's our world!

Dr. L. Harold DeWolf wrote in his book *A Hard Rain and A Cross*, "Because we Christians (we who call ourselves by the name of Christ) do not want to get involved in the reconciling way of the cross, the world itself moves as if in a kind of ritual dance toward death. Because Christians won't pick up the towel and basin, because Christians won't pick up the cross, because Christians won't follow Jesus—the world dances toward death."

One day, a couple of years ago, I picked up one of my sons who was fourteen years old, and competing in a track meet. As any busy father, I wasn't there but probably should have been when he ran the race; but I was there to pick him up. As he came out of the gate, I could see that he hadn't won. You know, you can tell the difference between a winner and a loser. That morning he had left and said, "Daddy, I feel great. I had a good night's sleep. I'm on training and I feel like I'll really do well today." He normally doesn't do very well in track. I think he has won two races in ten years. And that day as he came to the car I could see that it hadn't gone well, so I thought we would get it over with and said, "Son, how did you do?" And he replied, "The worst I have ever done." And I said, "Well, what went wrong? You thought you would do better." He said, "Well, you see, Daddy, it's like this. I run the 330 and in the Junior High School where I go we train on a 330 yard track. And here today the 330 yard race was staked out on a 440 yard course. And I misjudged the length of the race. I started off easy, saving myself. I started running real hard too late. The race was over too quick, and when the race was over, I had too much left. I hadn't used all I had." That's funny, but it's tragic. A picture of our world? Have we misjudged the race? Have we started off run-

ning too easy? *For what are we saving ourselves?* The race
could be over too quickly, and we could have too much left?
For what?

Sociologist Sorokin, historian Snow, theologian DeWolf, a
junior high school boy, a prison in Germany, a young widow on
a plane, war, racism, hatred, bitterness, defeat, grief, fear,
doubt! A look at our world. Is that where we are? I hope not.

Surely, as all of us look at our world we realize that there
must be change. And maybe that is what God is saying to us,
renewal and rebirth in the church, or further tragedy. There
must be change, there must be renewal, there must be redemption, there must be new faith in our time or further chaos will
come. Could it be the judgment of God? I'm not sure but that it is.

How can we achieve this new faith, this redemption? Can it
be achieved? I suppose this is what we are wrestling with.

Let us look at the possibilities, for a few moments. One of
the ironies of our time is that this age is proclaimed by many
leaders of our church to be the ecumenical age. Events taking
place in Amsterdam, Evanston, Geneva, Vatican I and II, are
evidences that this is the ecumenical age. At the same time,
though, it appears very clear to me that there is another fact,
right in our midst, in our church, in our world; there are more
theological irreconcilables than there have ever been in modern
history within the church. I hold the specter before you that,
while we talk about unity, schism and disunity are just beneath
the surface within the laity and the clergy; and, we are not
dealing with them as we ought.

As pastor, and now as a district superintendent, one of the
frustrating experiences of my life is, and has been, working with
what I would call traditional, Apostles' Creed-cultural Christians, who believe the right things but do not live out that faith
in life. These do not understand the full implications of the story
of the Good Samaritan, or of the Woman at the Well. They
have heard the words, "Come unto me," but have not heard the
words, "Go ye into the world." Is there any doubt that dead
orthodoxy, or even fundamental piety, will not answer the problems of our times, an orthodoxy which believes the right things
but does not live out that faith in and through the world. And,
somehow I think I would stand in the realm of the orthodox, but
an *uninvolved faith will not do!*

It is because of this real lack of living faith, more than anything else I believe, that thousands of young people are turning
from the church. And these young people are looking at us and
saying, "Do you measure up to what you say on Sunday morning
—do you carry it out in your life?"

I consider myself an evangelical Christian in the Wesleyan tradition, but I do not consider a dead orthodoxy to be in the Wesleyan tradition. Somehow we have got to change, and motivate and involve ourselves.

Now, I do not think that fundamentalistic theology is a live option for most of us today. I don't think we have any fundamental-orthodox-literalists here. I don't really think that such a theology is a viable option to many in our world today. It's surely not a live one in most of our churches. On the other hand, though, and I think this is something worth looking into a little bit deeper, we have a considerable, well-publicized and vocal group of so-called secular-oriented churchmen, who say that "man has come of age," that somehow man has outgrown the myth of God. Or as Albert Outler has so bitingly said, "They are more and more inclined to the thesis that, in the beginning, man created God to serve the human cause." And therefore we no longer need the myth that they created. Not in the beginning God, but in the beginning man. As I see it, there is in this theology the oldest of heresies—the deification of man and the humanization of God. Some persons seem to say, "For the first time in history man has advanced to the place where he can go it alone. Our intelligence has caught up with our times." *What arrogance! And what ignorance!* They do not read history. C. S. Lewis says that modern man thinks his head has grown larger but it really hasn't. It only looks larger due to the atrophy of the chest. Have these not heard of Adam in the garden, of the Gnostics that John wrote about, of the Docetists the early church dealt with, or even of Pelagius, the heretic, who preached in Rome from 401 to 409? And this is what he preached, if you will go back and search it out: Man, through his will and good works, through his involvement in society can change this world and can save this world. That's what Pelagius preached in 401 and 409. And it's more than just an ironic footnote in history that he left Rome in 409 and in 410 Alaric the vandal sacked Rome and burned it to the ground. History is replete with vignettes like this.

In a recent pastoral letter from the Roman Catholic Bishop of America it was stated, "A new Pelagianism seeks salvation in the correction of structure rather than in conversion to God." Let us correct structure, but let us not believe that salvation is there.

Many of us learned as schoolboys the poem "Invictus" . . . I remember, I declaimed it. I believed it. . . . "I am the master of my fate. I am the captain of my soul." What a fallacy! And what heresy that it was taught to schoolboys. The basic weakness of this theology is that it does not acknowledge original sin, or the fall of man, or perhaps "my sin." The need of man for a Saviour and a Redeemer! The secular movement is in many ways commendable. It's more commendable than Christians who won't get involved, let me affirm. But, because it does not, or will not allow, for a man's personal relationship with a very real and alive God, as revealed in Jesus Christ, as made known in the Holy Spirit, it is the author of the worst idolatry created in the world—*man's idolatry and worship of himself.*

There is not enough time to go into the historical bases of modern theology and the radical theologies of our day, but let me give you a look at a couple. The poet, William Blake, is the patron saint of the "death of God" theologians with his statement: "Thou art a man. God is no more." That's where that part of it began. But coincidentally, William Blake is also the patron saint of the Satan cult in San Francisco.

Hietsche and Hegel are the real fathers of secularism and they are also the philosophical fathers of "The Third Reich." They are the Fathers of Nazism, Dachau, and Plotzensee. The myth of the super-race was built upon their "man come of age." As I understand it, secularism is a theology of good works and not a gospel of redemption. For the secularist there is no such thing as personal salvation, personal forgiveness, personal redemption. What Jesus did, whatever that was, was for forgiveness, personal redemption. What Jesus did, whatever that was, was for the world and not for individual man. *I don't believe it!* As I understand secular involvement, without personal redemption, it is the desire to share with the ghetto, or with the inner-city or with the under-privileged man, part of the affluence of man. We want to share education, economic success, material prosperity, social acceptance, and political power. Now you see, these are the products and the gifts of affluence. They truly are. And least of all, or not at all, is a personal relationship with the Saviour, Jesus Christ important or possible. You are not supposed to mention that. The secularists would maintain that affluent man is the sickest part of our society, and with that I would agree. *Modern, affluent, urban culture is sick.* And yet, we seem to say we want to share a part of the sickness to help another man get well. As if this is the gospel! "There is a way that seems right unto a man and the ends thereof are the ways of death."

There are two TV commercials in our area, beamed to the affluent man and attesting to his frustration. Two beautiful television commercials showing pictures of lakes and golf courses and country clubs are entitled: "Run away to Runaway Bay" and "Hide away at Hideaway Lake." That's how healthy affluent culture is. Men are in need of a hiding place. It is my thesis, and I judge the biblical thesis, that man is selfish, that man is a sinning creature, *that man does need redemption, that man must be changed or remade into the image of our Saviour, as a servant child of God.*

It was Theodore Roosevelt who rather pungently commented upon the limitations of education when it was being held up as the real Messiah of his time, "If you take a man who steals from boxcars and educate him without changing his heart, he'll wind up stealing trains." That's still true.

The great plea of our time is for relevance. And I want to be relevant! All of us do! Yes, we make a plea for relevance. But, I sometimes think this means to say to modern man what he wants you to say, to confirm his ego and flatter his self-image, which is another way of saying "to identify with our age," or to join it. But I would remind you that he who marries the spirit of his own age is ever destined to be a widow in the next. *There is a Spirit and a truth that transcends any age.* If to be relevant then, is to join with dead orthodoxy of much of the church; or with the secular-activitist revolutionary; all of them without an obedient relationship to Jesus Christ as Saviour and Lord —*then I choose to be irrelevant,* and speak what I know to be the truth in my own experience. I have lived as a modern secular man. I lived there for fifteen years, as an oilman, a politician, a judge, as a man dealing with things and finding, finally, one day that there was a God who cared for me in Jesus Christ, and finding *there* a new way of life. There is no personal, or lasting social salvation apart from knowing Jesus Christ. *I know of none other.*

Well, I've said that pious, dead orthodoxy is a heresy. And I believe it. Secular activism without personal redemption is a heresy. And I believe it. What have we left? Where are we?

One definition of a heresy, and I think it is a good one, is that every heresy is a perversion of a great truth. A truth carried too far to the exclusion of another truth. That is, say, in the human-divine controversy about Jesus, carry either one of these too far and you have a heresy. Wesley, in his time, sought to bring two aspects of faith, "so long asunder" back together. Perhaps we are called to be Wesleyans again. He was called to bring back together "knowledge and vital piety." We must, in our day, unite again these two parts of a whole truth into the great truth of the New Testament: a personal relationship with a redeeming God without which man cannot be redeemed—and a vital concern with all of man in all of life every day. "Come unto me." "Go ye into the world." Or as Elizabeth O'Conner has said, "Journey Inward-Journey Outward."

Bishop Earl Hunt has said: "We seem to be trying to erect an ever expanding superstructure of social action upon a constantly diminishing foundation of religious faith in the Christian community in recent years." And he added, "Our social activism, with all of its Christian intentions, and its Christian nature, stands today upon the brink of a terrible bankruptcy if it is not again undergirded with the enthusiasm and faithful study of the word of God." I believe, with all my heart, that if we combine these two, and understand what we are doing, the need for repentance, the need for personal salvation, based upon Scripture, and God's clear command to involvement in the world, *the glory of it all,* my dear friends, is that it will work. And it is the only faith which will.

Jesus Christ still redeems! Still transforms! And makes disciples! God sent a Son to us, and all men, that we might be redeemed. Today, as in every day since that day, God seeks many sons to carry on the work as fellow heirs of his only Son. Incarnate, that's what it means—the Spirit of God in us. The glory of it all, is that I, Ira Galloway, sinner, can be a son of God, through Jesus Christ. And so can you! *What glory this! What joy! What wonder! What great good news! Amen.*

5

Confirmation and Church Renewal

by CARL L. STOCKING

The most naive member of the Christian family and the institutional church has come to realize that with rare exceptions Protestant Christian churches are floundering. One could spend a lot of time analyzing why this is so. This has already been done by many persons, many of whom are more capable than I. I will not attempt such a task but assume the reader is quite aware of our pluralistic society and its many problems.

I do want to mention one problem that I believe is a major weakness in the present Protestant membership recruiting and training program. Most Protestants have come into membership in a local church with little or no understanding of what the church is, of who he or she is as a person, what it means to be Christian, and most of all what it means to be a Christian in a pluralistic society like ours. Add to that a skimpy knowledge of the Bible with little encouragement to read or study the Book and you have a devastating situation.

As the above statements imply, it has become too easy to become a member of a particular local church. In the past, conversion experience, a desire to be a member, or an appearance at a church altar to answer a few questions which may not have been taken seriously were all that was required. As a result we have too many uncommitted church members. Some attempts were made at membership training but these, too, were often inadequate. The period of instruction was often too short and in too many instances was done in a way that seemed to indicate the person had learned little during his church school experiences and it all had to be done in membership training classes.

As part of an attempt at church renewal, confirmation has now come to play a greater part in the process of church membership. To put it simply, confirmation is that point in the growth and development of the church member when he assumes for himself and takes responsibility for the vows made at his bap-

Carl L. Stocking is a member of the staff of the Board of Education of The United Methodist Church. He is Director of Services to Pastors and District Superintendents.

tism, or that were made for him by the congregation and his
parents as a part of infant baptism.

The implications of confirmation are many: (1) Membership
training is a life-span activity, a task never completed. (2) Infant baptism is the initiation rite marking the individual as a
member of the Christian family. (3) The educational ministry
of the church carried on through the church school and all
other forms of group learning is part of membership training.
(4) The confirmation preparation class should be the time when
the individual is led to assume for himself the vows for confirmation and full membership in the church. (5) The ritual for
confirmation is the act where the new member witnesses before
God and the congregation his intention to accept and to dedicate
himself to follow the Christian way of life. He is then recognized
as a full member of The United Methodist Church. (6) As a
confirmed and full member the individual assumes the responsibility of citizenship in the Christian community. He will continue
to study and to grow in his citizenship responsibilities.

Thus, confirmation becomes a vital step in the member's development as a citizen in the Christian community. It is at this
point that evangelism and education go hand in hand. The goal
of every church school teacher should be to lead those whom
they teach into a Christian experience. This is also the goal of
evangelism.

The question has often arisen as to the age when decisions to
enter into full membership should be made. The answers cover
a wide range but there seems to be a general agreement that the
junior high age is the logical time. *The Book of Discipline* sug-
gests that those finishing the sixth grade would be acceptable
at the pastor's discretion. My observation is that it is during
the junior and senior high years that youth begin really to
wrestle with the question of who they are, to reject or to confirm
the Christian faith that has been presented to them during their
formative years. This should be the best age for a confirmation
of their faith.

All that I have discussed here can and does produce results.
Several years ago a church large enough to have an associate
pastor took a look at its ministry with youth and its inadequate
"membership training program." The wise senior pastor placed
the membership training program in the hands of his associate
and freed him from other tasks so that he could really give time
to develop an adequate program. He began his work with
a study of what was happening in "membership preparation"
not only in Methodism, but across Protestantism. His studies
led him to the position expressed in this article.

As he began his program he enlisted the support of both the Commission on Evangelism and the Commission on Education. He next enlisted the support of all church school teachers so that they saw themselves as part of the team preparing the children and youth, not only to have some understandings of their faith, but also to confirm that faith as their own. Another step was to enlist the cooperation of the parents. The work with the parents, as with church school workers, began with the baptism of the child and carried through to confirmation as to the door to "full membership" in the church.

As the young pastor got this program in operation he discovered that at the point of decision for full membership our Methodist program as generally practiced had left a vacuum. Little or nothing was done to prepare the youth for that decision. Taking a clue from some of our sister denominations, he concluded that confirmation as practiced in many denominations was the missing link in the process of membership training. This became the decision point for full membership in the church.

The preparation for this experience took a full year. Special studies were started over and above the regular study program of the church. Some of these involved weekend retreats with intensive periods of study. Others were done in longer camping experiences where issues of church membership could be discussed in a more informal setting. The whole year was spent in preparing the young person for that very important decision.

As the day designated as "membership Sunday" approached, each young person was given the opportunity to make his decision. No pressure was applied by parents, pastor, or friends. If he felt that he was not ready, his decision was accepted and further study programs were planned. For those making affirmative decisions, another study of the membership vows was made.

"Membership Sunday" was a gala affair. It was a day of joy and rejoicing for the member, the parents, and the congregation —a day never to be forgotten.

The lasting effects of this type of confirmation preparation and the confirmation act were many: (1) Church membership became more meaningful for the participants—confirmation was not just a perfunctory performance that seemed unimportant. (2) The act of confirmation confronted the participant with a decision to be made, a decision that he alone must make. (3) Infant baptism took on a new meaning in its relationship to confirmation and church membership. (4) The program involved parents, church school teachers, the Commissions on Evangelism and Education, and the congregation in preparing these persons for full membership in the church. These cooperative efforts made being a part of the Christian community a meaningful experience. (5) The persons who became full members through this kind of program seldom became drop-outs, a factor too prevalent in the church today. (6) They had at least a working knowledge of what the church is and their task as a member.

The most exciting experiences I have had over the past few years have been a number of Confirmation Preparation Laboratory Schools for pastors. What these have meant to pastors can best be expressed in the words of an older minister at the close of one of the labs: "Why couldn't I have had this experience thirty years ago?"

This is why I say that confirmation is related to church renewal. We must take Jesus Christ seriously and make church membership meaningful. God's kingdom will go on but he will need new prophets if we fail.

6

Let Us Save Souls

by ALLAN R. BROCKWAY

"I can't see that social action has anything to do with the church," a critic of Dr. Ralph Abernathy and the Poor Peoples' Campaign told me recently. "The church should get to work saving souls."

He was right. The business of the church is saving souls or, better, being the agent through which God saves souls. Unfortunately, however, we live in a day when the definition of a saved soul has become, at the very least, ambiguous. Consequently the role of the church as agent of salvation has become unclear. What does the church do when it sets out to save souls? How does it know whether it has been effective?

Part of our difficulty doubtless lies in the residue of the split between body and soul, which we inherited from early Greek thought. Accordingly, we operate (even when we consciously reject it) on the assumption that a man's soul may be saved while his body and his social health stagnate, at best, or degenerate, at worst.

Our difficulty lies also in a heritage in the church of concentration upon individuals to the exclusion of the social conditions that produced them. We have failed to take full cognizance of the social self, which acts with a will of its own that is independent of the millions of individual selves that comprise it.

It is the business of the church to be the agent through which the soul of society may be saved and the road eased for the salvation of individual souls. Social action on the part of the church is, in this context, an attempt to mediate God's saving grace to the social self—and no one should be surprised that the effort meets with resistance. No man and no society easily recognizes its need for salvation. Indeed, the suggestion that such is required is received as a threat to the society itself. But resistance is a poor reason for giving up the endeavor,

Allan R. Brockway is Director of the Office of Publications of the Board of Christian Social Concerns of The United Methodist Church. He is the editor of engage magazine, published by the Board of Christian Social Concerns. "Let Us Save Souls" first appeared in the July 15, 1969 issue of engage and is reprinted here with permission.

for failing to carry out the New Testament injunction to go into all the world with the saving possibility in Jesus Christ.

That saving word, for individuals, is that *you* may receive yourself as an absolutely significant human being. Reception of that possibility has been symbolized by the affirmation, "I believe in Jesus Christ as Lord and Savior." The saving word, for society, is that society may receive itself as fully significant *and* that all members of it may do also. Reception of that possibility is symbolized by the passage of legislation, the adoption of corporate practice, the active will of the people to the end that the Christ possibility be embodied in social existence.

But the salvation of society is hindered by resistance to change in favor of the gospel. All of us are part of this resistance, none may claim righteousness; no, not one. We all want what we want, even though others starve for food or social significance. And we are prepared to go to hell to keep and to get what we want. We have all sorts of "righteous" ways of treading the hellish path. And they most frequently come down to: "they" have no right to upset things. Jim Forman has no right to demand reparations. Ralph Abernathy has no right to invade Washington. Students have no right to disrupt universities. No one has the right to experiment with drugs. "Underground" papers have no right to use taboo language. Churchmen have no right— because they are *churchmen*—to support those who do these things.

Those of us who are interested in saving souls have a special responsibility to listen and heed these disparate voices within the social self. For they say the society is in need of salvation and they offer avenues for accomplishing that salvation. If their salvation looks like damnation, then we could do worse than study again the story of the rich young man's response to Jesus.

Before we shout that these dissident voices are not the voice of Jesus (and therefore may be safely repressed) we must remember the prophets' word that God acts in the Assyrians and the Babylonians, in the alien forces that wreak judgment on a sinful people who think themselves righteous.

When you get right down to it, the question has to be: Are we concerned to save souls *or* are we concerned to save ourselves?

7

Evangelism in Total Church Ministry

by H. THOMAS WALKER

The New Testament Church portrays a life style for the Body and a pattern for the task of evangelism. The work of evangelism is the axis around which the total life of the church revolved. The first expression of the church at her birth was the proclamation of the "Good News" of God's love revealed in the life, death and resurrection of Jesus of Nazareth. Jesus had commanded the disciples to "be witnesses" wherever they found themselves. Paul's missionary journeys were undertaken for the purpose of evangelism, to bring "Good News" to every person. It was not a matter of the church being concerned for "mission" or "evangelism"; evangelism *was* the mission.

Somehow through the two thousand years of church history, evangelism has been separated from the main stream of its life. This dichotomy probably had some of its origins in the days of revivalism in America when the task of evangelism was in large measure the responsibility of the "professional" evangelist. Such a distortion of the responsibility for evangelism can be traced to the clergy-laity heresy. Whereas the clergy assumed more and more responsibility for the basic work of the church: evangelism, worship/fellowship and service, the laity assumed less and less. (In the New Testament the functions of worship and fellowship seem to be almost synonymous with each other. We have tended to think that we worship upstairs and fellowship downstairs. The early church seemed to have such an awareness of the presence of the living God that they worshipped every time they came together. They seemed to have such love for each other that they had fellowship when they worshipped. It might be described in this fashion: When they had the sacrament they had a party. When they had a party they had the sacrament.)

H. Thomas Walker is superintendent of the Northwest District, Minnesota Conference of the United Methodist Church. He has served as a pastor, a chaplain, and a staff member of the General Board of Evangelism of the United Methodist Church.

As the clergy assumed larger responsibility for the task of the church, it was natural that they were expected to be the evangelists for the church. While evangelists are mentioned three times in the New Testament, there was probably no sharp distinction between them and other apostles in those days. It was only one more step to the professional among the professionals, the "evangelist" of the nineteenth and first half of the twentieth centuries. In the latter half of the twentieth century we have a new breed of professional evangelist. He is the urban or inner city minister, hired by the church to go and "be" (the witness) where the church as a body has been unwilling to go.

Just as worship/fellowship and service are a part of the very life of the church, evangelism must not be considered an adjunct to the work of the church, to be the church is to be about the task of evangelism. Proclaiming the "Good News" is not a function of the "professional," or the clergy, nor is it the responsibility of a small group within the life of the church. The work of evangelism involves the total Body. It is an emphasis which spans the year and is not confined merely to a season or a specified period of time.

The above is not meant to suggest that there should be no times of special emphasis on evangelism or that certain persons should not be selected to be responsible to plan for the work of evangelism within the local church. Someone has correctly said, "Everyone's business is no one's business." The work area on evangelism must not be abandoned, but its emphasis must be redirected. It has to assume responsibility for involving the total membership in this basic function of the church.

As soon as you begin to move in this direction, you are confronted with the fact that many church members find the work of evangelism repugnant to them. At one period in history, evangelism was undertaken as a means of "saving" persons from the fires of hell. As the fear of hell became less significant to Americans, the church gradually became involved in evangelism that emphasized the "good" to be found in being related to the organizational church. As Americans have become less impressed with the help that comes from this relationship, evangelism has very often been undertaken as a means of getting new members and financial support for the church and for the service it seeks to render.

The style of evangelism resulting from these motives, as well as the motives themselves, greatly influences the willingness of the total membership to involve itself in the work of evangelism in the present day. Thus one of the first steps needed is to help the church define an evangelism which will be effective and authentic in today's world. This will best be done by looking far beyond the immediate past history to the Biblical origins of the function of evangelism. *New Testament evangelism does not center on salvation from hell in the hereafter, but rather on the fullness of life for now. It does not promise to make you "good" by coming into the fellowship of the church; the fellowship of the church seeks to open the goodness of God's love for you. It does not seek to bring you into the body for the sake of the church, it seeks to bring you into the body for the sake of your total being.*

As the people of the church begin to sense that evangelism is not a program to get new members for the sake of the church, but for the sake of a ministry to the persons to whom the Evangel (Good News) is presented, there is much more willingness to be involved in the task. When Peter and John went to the gate called Beautiful and met the man who was crippled who asked alms, they served his needs, but the service itself became an occasion of evangelism. Peter said, "I have no silver and gold, but I give you what I have; in the name of Jesus of Nazareth, walk." (Acts 3:6) On some occasions there have been those who have used service as a means of entrée to impose the Evangel on the person served. This process tended to be unsatisfactory for evangelism and the worth of the service was, to a degree, negated. On the other hand, the object of Christian love is not to do something "nice" for another person so much as it is to help that person come to the place where he too can express love. Since the Christian finds fulfillment in serving, if he would really serve it is his object to help the person served to become a servant. With this understanding the inclusion of the proclamation of "Good News" with the service is not only acceptable but mandatory. The service that does not include the possibility of the source of love for the one who is loved as well as for the lover, is less than the greatest service. An expression of love that does not include the service that is needed is not love at all.

The early church seems to have taken the position of responding to their task with this in mind. As indicated earlier, service and proclamation (evangelism) seemed to be expressed simultaneously. They did not see themselves as being involved in service at one point and evangelism at another, but rather, they saw the two as a natural expression of their lives as the people of God to the world outside of the body of Christ. As their lives expressed God's love for the world they sought to help that same world discover God's love as it had been revealed in Jesus Christ.

As the church considers its total life from within, it must be aware that it exists for this reason. In other words, the worship/ fellowship (the intra-personal relationships within the church that include instruction, organizational work, support and discipline of each other, etc.) need to be designed with the recognition of this two-fold responsibility (service and proclamation —evangelism) to the world. The plans for the service and proclamation must be expressed in combination as evangelism. Not long ago I worked in a church in which the white congregation located in the black ghetto had had a rather comprehensive service center for the community, but no expression of the Evangel to the community. Some of the people of the community began to say to the church, "You want to do things for us, but you do not invite us to join you in your church." Strangely, some of the people were a little amazed that there should be this kind of reaction.

To move this one step further along the way, the church which fails to include in its evangelistic thrust a social consciousness is not really expressing God's love for the world. The concern that Jesus expressed for man, was a concern that included the whole man. When he drove the money changers out of the temple, he was striking at a social institution. When Paul pleaded for the release of Onesimus, he was moving against slavery, a social institution. If the Twentieth-Century church is to be faithful to its task, it must be aware of the social structures that are destructive to persons. By the same token the social consciousness that does not include the "Good News," falls short of the demands placed upon it by the New Testament. We cannot afford the luxury of narrow evangelism or limited social concern. The full measure of the impact of the gospel is essential to meet the needs of the Twentieth-Century man. This is the task assigned to the church for this day.

For many churches this holistic approach to the task of the church will mean a redefining of the work of the church. With the new structure for the local United Methodist Church, this is an excellent time to see that the proclamation of the "Good News" is made an integral part of the total life of the whole church (i.e., Women's Society of Christian Service, UMYF, church school, work areas). The Council on Ministries is charged with fulfilling this function. The foundation for their work needs to be carefully established so they see the broad implications of what it is to be the church. For some groups and individuals it will be a matter of helping them redefine their concept of evangelism to include service and a social consciousness. In other settings, the concepts of service and social consciousness will need to be expanded to include evangelism. In every situation there needs to be constant awareness that we are called to be "God's people" in today's world.

Once the Council on Ministries has begun to define the ministry of the particular church, the chairmen of the various work areas or commissions, age-level coordinators and groups within the church need to establish their program plans with the overall mission of the church in mind. This kind of direction is so commonplace that it seems redundant to suggest it as the pattern, yet the church has for so long operated as fragmented commissions and groups going off in somewhat harmonious but differing directions. For instance, seldom does the church school feel responsible for the evangelistic task of the church, yet it can and ought to be a vital part of that particular concern. Likewise, the commission on evangelism does not consider itself responsibly involved in the social concerns of the church.

The New Testament describes the church as a body, with each of the parts making a contribution to the responsibility of the total. Similarly, this idea is a part of the design of The United Methodist Church. For instance, the 1968 *Book of Discipline* states, "The purpose of the Women's Society of Christian Service and Wesleyan Service Guild shall be to help women grow in the knowledge and experience of God as revealed in Jesus Christ, to challenge them to respond to God's redemptive purpose in the world, to unite them in a Christian fellowship to make Christ known throughout the world, and to develop a personal responsibility for the whole task of the church." (Par. 159) United Methodist Youth Fellowship and United Methodist Men have similar responsibility for the total task of the church.

The structure adopted at the 1968 General Conference allows for and seeks to assure unanimity of purpose. This is crucial. (It is never helpful for members of a body to ride off in all directions at once.) However if this unified approach to the church's task is to be as useful as it can and should be, it will be necessary for the leadership of the church to be faithful and responsible in determining the direction the church is to take. This will be accomplished by the leadership of the church involving as much of the membership as possible in determining how the church will minister. Unfortunately, few of us have been willing to operate in this fashion in the past. Instead, we have tried to develop a program and then sell it to the church officials and the general membership.

This pattern of program development is not very effective at this moment in history. The program that is developed within the church is the one that is most apt to win broad support

from the church. As humans we seem to feel most responsible
for those things which we own. This same thing is a dynamic
force in the matter of programs. When a group has a feeling of
ownership of a program, they will be more responsible than
when they feel that it belongs to someone else and is being
imposed upon them.

Involving people in the determination of direction is not only
more effective, it is more faithful to the New Testament idea
of the church as a body, a single unit. While we cannot suppose
that we must arrive at total unanimity of the expression of
purpose, there must be a general agreement of purpose or the
body will tend to pull itself to pieces.

Once this general direction of ministry has been determined,
the various parts of the body must assume responsibility for
accomplishing this purpose. It is the responsibility of the Council
on Ministries to help the various parts maintain awareness of
the general direction and the total task. This function is of
crucial significance in the life of the church. No one part must
see itself as the whole. Of equal importance, each part must be
concerned for the health of the whole body. The whole cannot
be complete if some of the parts are neglected.

Evangelism that is less than central to the total life of the
church is a distortion. It will not be effectively expressed by the
professional working alone, whether he be the revivalist or the
inner-city worker. It will not be effectively accomplished by the
pastor or a small group of persons within the church. It is
best accomplished when it becomes the natural expression of the
total life of the church as a body and as the people express in
their total existence "Good News," the unmerited love of God
as it is revealed in Jesus Christ.

8

Are We Listening?
by HAROLD ROGERS

A young serviceman was asked why he regularly attended the Sunday morning worship services held in the post chapel. His reply, "I go to get something to help me through the week until I can go back and get some more."

A minister in a district workshop asked those present, "How many of you have been hurt by the church?" Without exception every person in the group raised a hand.

Christ United Methodist Church in Bethel Park, Pennsylvania recently held a feed-back forum where the question was asked, "What does my commitment to Christ really mean to me?" Over five hundred replies were received.

How long has it been since we as members of the church have asked this or similar questions of ourselves and of our fellow members? And if we have asked them, have we honestly listened to the answers given?

Politicians ask questions of their constituents and listen. Businessmen ask questions of their customers and listen. Radio and television networks ask questions and listen to their viewers. But are we, as a church, concerned enough about our members to ask questions and listen?

Some of the questions to which we might address ourselves are:

1. Do our members, new and old, know what it means to make a full commitment to Jesus Christ as Lord and Savior?

2. Do the members (myself included) reveal Christ in the way we live?

3. Do we know what percentage of our membership attends worship services regularly?

4. Does our congregation use any one of the several possible methods each Sunday to ascertain the attendance of individual members? Is this handled in such a way that those who are interested in the ministry to members and visitors

Harold Rogers is the Director of Discipleship Cultivation for the General Board of Evangelism of The United Methodist Church. He is the author of *Live Coals, Neighborhood Action Plan,* and *Witnessing Where You Are,* published by TIDINGS.

can tell on Monday morning which of those for whom they
are responsible were present and which were not? If such
a check is made are the names given to interested members
who might take the time to make a personal inquiry of
these persons and ascertain their reasons for attending or
not attending? These questions would not be phrased as a
mechanical survey, but rather should come as a demonstration of personal interest and concern.

5. Do our church school teachers attend the worship services
   regularly? Do they encourage their pupils to attend?

A group of persons, carefully selected and adequately trained,
could obtain answers to many of the questions listed, and perhaps offer a valid ministry at that time. But once the answers
are obtained and studied remedial steps may be taken that would
prove beneficial to both the individual and the entire congregation.

As we look at the early church described in The Acts of the
Apostles we discover that in those days the world was turned
upside down because:

1. The church was a fellowship whose members cared for one
   another.
2. It was a fellowship that worshiped together with a real
   sense of expectancy.
3. They believed that the Spirit of the living God was truly
   present in their midst.
4. They prayed believing.
5. With complete dedication they went out to serve and to say,
   "Jesus is Lord."

In a survey conducted by the American Lutheran Church
among the several pertinent facts ascertained as to why church
members become inactive, are:

1. A feeling of not being wanted.
2. The church is too class conscious.
3. Self-consciousness about the inability to make what is considered an adequate contribution to the church, plus a re-
   sentment of what seems to be unreasonable demands by the
   church—the church having failed to give adequate explana-
   tion and motivation.
4. The church's failure to communicate in laymen's language.
5. Program of the church dull, lifeless, uninviting.
6. Lack of adequate knowledge of God, Christ, man, sin and
   the church.
7. Personal grievances, misunderstandings or differences involving the minister, church leadership, an organization,
   an individual member.

What can we do?
1. We can ask and listen.
2. We can attend and invite others *to come with us.*
3. We can give to the best of our ability because God has given to us. We are only stewards of our possessions.
4. We can develop an effective parish plan enlisting carefully selected individuals who are willing to take training and develop a vital relationship with their neighbors.

The church in action is a going, growing, meaningful church. It relates to persons as they face the challenges of the world in which they take a daily part. People want to be where the action is and the living church is action—life changing action.

Definitely we remember that the church is of God, but it includes people—you and me, our hopes, our hungers, our joys, our disappointments, our frustrations, our work and our play. It is not perfect even after two thousand years, but it is the only fellowship with the express purpose of transmitting the love of God from generation to generation—that is the miracle that has kept it alive.

As we listen to God, we listen to our church, and we listen to our neighbors expectantly, hopefully, prayerfully. Having listened, we share those things that we personally have discovered, that the "Good News" from God is reconciliation. "From first to last this has been the work of God. He has reconciled us men to himself through Christ, and he has enlisted us in this service of reconciliation." (II Corinthians 5:18 NEB)

9

Witnessing Through The News Media or For Christ's Sake, Get The News Out

by CARL E. KEIGHTLEY

A book on the shelves of a book store caught my eye. Its title was *Parson To Parson*. The saleslady smiled when I remarked, "Well, I see the preachers are talking to themselves again." My remark was half in jest. We do need to talk among ourselves, to nurture our people. But there was meaning in the jest too. One of the problems of the church these days is that we are spending too much time talking to ourselves. We are much better at nurturing than we are at witnessing.

A young minister I know said some things on television that set off a furor in his town. Some thought he was a hero. Some thought he was a rash and irresponsible young man. A case could have been made for both points of view. But there was one point of view expressed that is utterly indefensible. Some said it would have been all right for him to say it to his own people, but not on television. Not so. Either he ought not have spoken the word from the pulpit at all or it ought to be spoken to all men everywhere. Can you imagine John Wesley doing anything but rejoicing at the thought that from any single pulpit on any single Sunday, the world could become a preacher's parish?

Newsmen do not always please me by what they choose to proclaim about our society, nor do I always agree with their interpretations of what the church is doing or not doing, but we can be grateful that the press, both printed and electronic, often listens in on the church and even when we ignore it or resist it, it saves us from simply engaging in conversation among ourselves. We can be glad the public media sometimes "bugs"

Carl E. Keightley is Director of Communications for the General Board of Evangelism of The United Methodist Church. He is a former editor of the *Texas Methodist*.

our pulpits and committee rooms and proclaims to the world what we say and do.

But we ought not to leave all the initiative up to the press. The plain facts are that Christian denominations are neither providing the money nor the staff to make effective use of the mass media for the proclamation of the gospel. It is questionable whether or not Christians will ever provide the money to do the job that ought to be done in mass communications if they depend on denominational offices alone. It must be done at the grass roots by professionals who are willing to volunteer their know-how to the church. The really significant news is made in the local community if it is made at all. And even if the big news about the church is made at a national office, it will not get much attention without a local angle or grass roots touch at Dearborn, or Decatur, or Dixon, or Duckwater.

My first observation then is this: We must quit waiting for the mass media to bug our pulpits and committee rooms. We must take the initiative to make it easier for them to help us proclaim the good news of God as it is seen in the work and word of the local congregations who are committed to Jesus Christ as Lord. We proclaim it because it is our business to proclaim. When we make the public media's task easier, they make ours more effective.

We have a second reason for recognizing the need for a massive effort on the part of the church to make more effective use of radio, television, and the printed word. To put it bluntly: the church is dropping behind and ministers are growing weary from frustration. Every statistical release confirms this.

Some trace this failure to a lack of understanding of the mission of the church. But there never has been a day when so many ministers and laymen were so seriously seeking to understand the mission of the church.

Some lay the church's problems to its failure to be involved in the burning issues of the day. Nothing could be further from the truth. The church has never been so buffeted because of its relevance than it is today.

Some question the energy and commitment of the pastor. Paradox though it is, preachers have never been so comfortably housed and fed and entertained, and yet so diligent in their work or committed to their task.

Some point to disenchantment with the church's institutional life, but no responsible group of laymen would seriously propose that we close our schools, our hospitals, our homes for the children and the aged.

Some say we are programmed to death. But let a group of

pastors meet over a cup of coffee or be assigned to a committee and they come up with another program. And if the pastor pares the program, the laymen will find ways to fill their time with concoctions of their own, or join another club.

Some place the blame on sub-Christian lives. Hasn't there always been that?

The element we seldom look at is the problem of effectively communicating the gospel to the people of the world. The truth is that mass communications have spawned a secular world. Secularity is not necessarily evil. The world is God's gift, and we need to learn how to live in it as Christians and relate to it through its own channels of communication. Mass communications is a magnificent gift God has given to this generation. Unless we learn how to use it instead of cuss it, the church will lose the opportunity to be the cutting edge in society.

Modern business has been much smarter than the church. Through the use of mass communications, it has built a market for its products. In 1900 almost nobody was building automobiles. Today a million people are in the automobile factories and they are backed up by thousands more in related industries. But auto production and usage today would be only a meager fraction of what it is if the automobile industry had waited for Mr. Jones to tell Mr. Smith that Mr. Ford's automobile was good. People own automobiles today because of mass marketing through mass communications.

To be more accurate, we probably should refer to pickles instead of Fords. The comparison fits religion better. A Ford moving about the country would in some measure advertise itself. But if we had waited until Mrs. Jones told Mrs. Smith that Mr. Brown's pickles are good, we would still be in the pickle barrel stage at the crossroads grocery.

Modern manufacturers do not expect their retail outlets to sell their products without backing up their point of sales effort with mass communications about the product. Yet, in the church, we put the whole weight of the effort on the back of the preacher at (if you will not get your dander up at the comparison) the point of sales, the retail outlet. The retail man in the church has done an exceptionally good job. Generally, he has outdone the Avon lady for door to door effectiveness.

Our laymen have done a good job too. They've knocked on doors. And they are no slouches when it comes to improving the image of the church by providing attractive point-of-sales outlets. We have air-conditioning, foam-rubber cushions, beautiful and functional buildings. The laymen spend millions of dollars to build the church's image at the point of sales.

And yet I am amazed at how many times I drive into a town, even a small one, and a local filling station operator or a man on the street can't direct me to a local Methodist outlet. Point-of-sales operation in a modern competitive world just isn't enough. Our retail outlets (the local church) are working hard. If the church is slipping behind in its evangelism, it is because we are not opening enough retail outlets and backing them up with an effective program of communications.

When a national brewery discovered their sales *gain* (not their sales, but their annual *gain*) dropped 1.7 per cent they immediately launched a new $12 million advertising campaign. They did not seek to solve the problem by product research; they stepped up their communications.

This is not to suggest the church ought to avoid product research, but the fact is we have been giving major attention to product research (self-analysis) for a long time now and haven't yet substantially changed the tide. There might be some theological intricacies that need a little polishing and a lot of organizational restructuring is called for, but at the point where theory meets life, the church looks like a pretty good product to me.

Working with mass media is not a cure-all, but it offers *some* hope and *another* path into the hearts and minds of men that we have not yet sufficiently explored. (Recent surveys by Syracuse University showed that religious news in the secular press is well read.) All channels of mass communication offer an opportunity to support the difficult point-of-sales job our ministers and laymen undertake.

The church has both an advantage and a disadvantage over business in its use of mass communications. We do not have the money that business has. We do not operate for profit. This means we must depend on grass roots action rather than expecting the general church to do the job for us. But the public media recognizes that religion is a vital constructive force in the community. Naturally, they wish we would buy more time and space, and we should experiment in pay television and radio that pays for itself. But their newspapers and stations are also open to us without charge both through public service time and in the area of news. Let's learn how to help them help us.

Every minister ought to want to make his proclamation to as many people as he can. He may not be able to write, but he can stimulate his people in the local church to practice a vital Christianity and then *he can see that it is reported.* No man is embarrassed about desiring a wider ministry and hoping for a larger church. He should have no embarrassment therefore about making a wider witness through radio, television, and news-papers if he is seeking thereby to witness to the good news of God in Christ and not to himself. The public media may not be interested in what he has to *say* if he is not a Mr. Somebody, but if he does something fresh and vital for Christ's sake, they will be glad to bear witness to that.

We have never had a better day for communicating the gospel. The public press has learned that religion is news and is willing to publish that news. It would be tragic if the best we could do is to use the mass media to list sermon topics and report ladies' teas. Let us make news as we bring out congregations to deal with the burning issues of the day in the light of the gospel; as we become a reconciling agent in a fragmented world and as we claim men for service in Jesus' name and spirit. And having made news, let us report it for Christ's sake.

Except for sermons on radio and TV, relatively little is being done at the local level to use mass media for the proclamation of the Good News. In fact, when it comes to confronting the listener or viewer with the real issues of religion, secular men using secular media do a better job than churches do. For this, the church can be grateful. However, it is still foolish, or lazy, or stingy to expect the secular media to initiate or bear the expense for top grade handling of religious themes. Happily, here and there one finds a few efforts being made to make significant use of mass media.

TEEN PROGRAM

Many communities are now using "The Place." Designed by TRAFCO to relate the gospel in a meaningful way to teen-agers, the thirty minute radio program originates locally, fea-tures an adult host and three to five local teens as panelists. Between top forty recordings the panel briefly explores the social, moral, ethical, and theological implications of the thought presented in the musical selections. The purpose is to encourage teen-agers to become aware of the significance and meaning of life through his own music. Information on "The Place" is avail-able through TRAFCO, 1525 McGavock, Nashville, Tennessee.

DISTRICT MEN

Claude Whitehead, a United Methodist district superintendent in Alabama, has enlisted the men of the district to support a weekly thirty minute broadcast. Format includes a bulletin of local church activities, a brief message by a minister or layman, and a five minute interview on some phase of the church's wit-ness or program. The interview, says the superintendent, serves as a discussion starter for laymen of various denominations on their jobs in the plants. Mr. Whitehead also tapes a five minute program called "Crossroads," which is used in three communities on the district. Messages are three minutes, fifty seconds preceded and followed by announcements and music. The three minute format was chosen because radio men said, "If you wish to talk to persons who agree with you, have a fifteen minute or half-hour program. If you wish to talk to others, have a five minute program. Most persons will listen to anything for five minutes rather than switch stations." Cost of the daily program is a little over fifty dollars a week.

TV SERIES

Rev. Robert F. Larson and the Pennsylvania Council of Churches worked with WITF-TV in Hershey, Pennsylvania (Channel 13) to produce two month-long weekly programs on religion. Funds came from a Ford Foundation grant. "A Time To Act" was shown in April 1968 and "Is Religion Obsolete" was shown in February 1969. The communities in the viewing area were urged to complete the series throughout the month by obtaining special speakers for service clubs and other groups.

RECORD PROVIDED

The Minnesota Television, Radio, and Film Commission headed by its chairman, Rev. B. J. Stemme of Byron, Minnesota, prepared a seven inch record containing four commercials and mailed them to radio stations inviting them to use them on public service time. A self-addressed, postage paid card was enclosed on which the station could indicate when the spots would be used.

The Commission backed up the mailing with a letter to ministers in towns having a radio station. They were asked to encourage the use of the record. The sixty second spots used contemporary music like *Mrs. Robinson, Simple Simon,* and *God is Alive* and a brief spoken message.

NEWSPAPER CAMPAIGN

The Southern California-Arizona Conference undertook a broad-scale advertising program in behalf of the Christian community in six metropolitan areas. A series of thirteen messages appeared a total of 164 times in ten newspapers published in Los Angeles, San Diego, Phoenix, Tucson, Las Vegas, and Honolulu. Some appeared on news pages, others in such sections as sports, entertainment, financial, home decoration, and grocery advertisements. None appeared on the weekend church pages because the messages were aimed at the nonchurchman who spends little or no time reading the church page. Mats and repros were made available to local churches who might wish to run them in the smaller dailies or weeklies. Methodist Information was sponsor of the campaign.

The Denver area built a series of newspaper ads around "Men of Methodism in Colorado." After a description of the public and private life of the man, the ad says, "The Methodist Church builds men, who in turn build character into the men of the next generation. It is a cycle you can be a part of. There is a Methodist Church near you that would be most happy to welcome you 'into the family' . . . tomorrow!" Readers are invited to call Methodist Information for information about the fifty Denver District Churches.

Some churches are picking up the suggestion of the American Bible Society to use editorials to encourage Bible reading and get across a religious message. Sometimes the editorials are signed; sometimes they are not. The society, located at 1865 Broadway, New York, New York, has published a brochure to aid planning and placing editorials.

SPONSORS FOOTBALL BROADCAST

The 105 member United Methodist congregation at Clarksdale, Arizona underwrote one-quarter sponsorship of the high school football games on Radio Station KVIO in Cottonwood at a cost of $40 a week. The Worship Commission chairman, Duane Kirby owner and general manager of the station, wrote the commercials. As listeners throughout Arizona tuned in, they would hear commercials like this:

"What does church mean to you? Is it a place to go on Sunday morning when the golf course is too wet, or the weather's not right for fishing?

"Or is it a source of comfort and guidance? A spiritual uplifting home for you and your family?

"And how relevant is God in your scheme of things? Today's Christ is the same Christ that saw the world through the dark ages! To see how Christ is a relevant part of today's living, take your place alongside your neighbor this Sunday at the Clarksdale Community United Methodist Church. Then join the many groups working hard to put today's problems into the right perspective. There are youth fellowships, a Young at Heart Couple's Club, Bible Study groups, and many more sources of hope for every member of your family. If you really want something meaningful from life, attend church this Sunday with your family."

10

The Parable of the Continuing Carnival

by LEE RANCK

One Sunday night a mass of people streamed from hundreds of colorful, noisy sideshows and thronged to the Carnival's center stage for the long-awaited feature attraction. At 10:56 P.M. the lights dimmed; the crowds hushed, then watched in moonstruck silence as the Carnival unfolded its out-of-this-world extravaganza.

"That's one small step for man, one giant leap for mankind." Garbled words and pictures thrilled the awed watchers. Many hours later, when the show ended, the Carnival crowds began to dance and sing for joy. It had been magnificent, really spectacular, by far the best show that the Carnival had produced in many moons, worthy of the time and money which had gone into its production.

Only a few persons ignored the celebration—a frail child greedily gobbling table scraps at a sidewalk cafe, a young, pregnant woman sobbing over pictures at the Vietnam pavilion, an Egyptian and Israeli shouting curses at each other, a pickpocket sneaking through the entranced crowd, a cluster of hip youth doing their own thing.

"Now we can do anything we want to do," someone shouted, and the people echoed those words. Then a man tossed several coins on to the stage, others followed his act, and soon piles of silver and copper covered the wooden floor.

The frenzied dancing continued in a long line led by the show's producer, Brownwerner, and leading actor, Strongarm. As they snaked around the Carnival grounds, the people sang: "We can do anything we want to do; we'll visit Mars by '82." Moving past the Carnival's center stage, the people pitched more coins on the growing silver piles.

When the celebrators continued to dance and chant and throw

Lee Ranck is Director of Communications for the Board of Christian Social Concerns of The United Methodist Church. "The Parable of the Continuing Carnival" was first published in the August 1, 1969 issue of *engage* magazine, published by the Board of Christian Social Concerns of The United Methodist Church. It is reprinted here with permission.

their money center stage, Carnival workers at the sideshows began to grimace and mumble among themselves. Everyone was dancing past them, ignoring their beckoning displays and games, leaving no coins in their boxes. That feature event had completely overshadowed all the other Carnival activities.

But the people danced on—past the pavilion where Black Panthers sold hotcakes and sausage; past the target booths where a quarter bought three shots at a Viet Cong, Arab Commando or Biafran rebel; past the birth control exhibit where men, convinced by graphic displays, could enter a tent-clinic for the simple operation to end their reproductive liability; on past the pollution center where brave Carnival-goers could get a frightening look at scarred and tattered mother earth. The people flowed by the hundreds of side shows, ignoring them in the glow of that captivating main feature.

Finally one of the hawkers, a long-haired boy working at the Youth Pavilion, became disgusted with the continuing celebration. He ran to the Carnival's central power box and pulled a handle throwing the entire grounds into darkness. The dancing people stumbled and their cheers became shrieks. Then the youth turned the lights back on; amid the confusion he grabbed the Carnival's master mike and shouted a trite little ditty:

"We can do anything we want to do; we can stop the war, build great cities too; we can bring justice to all, end poverty's pain; educate our young, reverse earth's drain. We can do anything we want to do—if we don't do these things, then we're all through."

The youth continued to shout his rhyme through the loudspeaker until several policemen came and dragged him away. But the interruption had disturbed the celebration and the dancing and singing stopped. On the Carnival's center stage, attendants with push-brooms swept the coins into wheelbarrows and carted them away. Some of the people wandered out the main gate chattering about the good and bad parts of the main feature. Others entered the side shows, listening and reading and playing and sometimes leaving a little more of their money.

High in the air a father and small son looked out over the Carnival grounds as their swaying seat swung through the orbit of a mammoth ferris wheel.

"How long will the Carnival last, Daddy?" the child asked breathlessly as they dropped down toward the earth.

"Son, I guess that depends on the people," the father answered. "You know, we really can do anything we want to do. If we want, the Carnival could last forever. Or, it could end tomorrow."

11

Evangelism Among Spanish-Speaking Americans

by ROBERTO ESCAMILLA

There are at least 12,000,000 Spanish-speaking people in the United States. The main areas which are heavily populated by this minority group could be roughly distributed as follows: Texas, 3,000,000; California, 2,000,000; Metropolitan New York, 1,100,000; New Mexico, 380,000; Florida, 400,000; Arizona, 260,000; and the rest of them scattered over various regions in the Continental United States. It can be stated that there is hardly a city larger than 100,000 population that does not have a recognizable Spanish-speaking group.

The first Spanish-Americans in the U.S. were not immigrants at all, but were acquired people taken over in territorial acquisitions. They and their ancestors have been living on this land for some 200 years. About 85% of the total population is native born.

In addition, there has been an almost constant immigration from Mexico, Puerto Rico, and other Latin American countries. The Puerto Ricans have been U.S. citizens since 1917. Cubans have been arriving in Miami by the thousands since the Castro revolution. At least one-fourth of the population of Miami (around 300,000) is Cuban.

It is estimated that 20,000 Puerto Ricans are coming into this country each year while 40,000 Mexicans cross the border yearly.

The Spanish-speaking group is not as homogeneous as is popularly supposed, but it is made up of persons with a wide range of physical and cultural characteristics. Many have blond or red hair, blue eyes, and fair skin. Many are quite dark with black hair and black or brown eyes. Some are unskilled migrant

Roberto Escamilla is the Director of Bilingual Ministries on the Staff of the General Board of Evangelism of The United Methodist Church. He has served as a pastor and as a staff member of the Board of Missions of The United Methodist Church. He is the author of Spanish-language tracts published by Tidings.

workers, owning nothing, living in poverty. Some are highly trained technicians and professionals whose homes are indistinguishable from those of their Anglo colleagues and fellow workers. Some speak only Spanish; some know no Spanish and speak only English, but the highest percentage are bilingual.

Next to the Negro, the Spanish-speaking people are the largest minority group in the United States.

Perhaps some of the most dramatic statistics are the ones which have reference particularly to the migrant farm workers:

—Infant mortality: 125 per cent higher than national rate
—Maternal mortality: 125 per cent higher than national rate
—Influenza and pneumonia: 200 per cent higher than national rate
—Tuberculosis and other infectious diseases: 260 per cent higher than national rate
—Accidents: 300 per cent higher than national rate
—Life expectancy: 49 years[1]

Besides all the basic necessities of this minority group, such as a sense of acceptance, organization and leadership of their community life, education and health, there is the imperative necessity of their spiritual welfare.

It has been estimated that approximately 80% of the ten million Spanish-speaking people in the United States are unchurched.

The basic question needs to be asked: Is it possible to relate the plight of the Spanish-Americans to evangelism and the whole mission of the church? Is it related at all?

The answer is "No" if we think of evangelism merely as old-fashioned "revivalism" and if we think of the mission of the church as that which takes place only within its four walls.

But the answer is a categorical "Yes" if we understand evangelism as the whole process of healing and restoration and making people whole, the kind of evangelism that goes beyond the realm of personal salvation and penetrates into the realm of social concern and action; the kind of evangelism that is changing, creative and dynamic, and which is willing to "let the world set the agenda" or, better still, as Dr. Joseph Yeakel has stated, "Let the world *be* the agenda." The *Position Paper* of the General Board of Evangelism of The United Methodist Church has stated it well when it asserts that "man's predicament comes not only from his personal sin but also from his involvement in a sinful society. Evils such as racism, poverty and war do issue from the heart but also derive their massive power from

---

[1] Statistical data obtained from *Migration Today*, Div. of Inter-Church Aid, Refugee and World Service, World Council of Churches, Spring 1969.

social structures which must be identified and brought before the judgment of God."

In other words, if evangelism is to be relevant to our time, we need to be concerned not only with man's personal sin and his need for redemption, but also with the guilt of man in condoning social structures that enslave people in the captivity of social and spiritual ghettos.

The church can no longer ignore the plight of Spanish-Americans. The response of the church to their needs must be expressed through some tangible evidence of service and involvement. There are many communities, particularly in the Southwest and many other cities in America, which are heavily populated by people of Hispanic descent. Many of them have been virtually ignored by the church.

The time has come for the church to become dead serious about this significant segment of the population and to find ways to witness and to serve in each local community.

No one can deny that one of the "signs of our time" is the restlessness and ferment which is being evidenced in the ranks of this minority group. It may be identified as a kind of awakening of the so called "Silent Minority." Undoubtedly, a significant phase of the mission of the church today is precisely to listen to the cries of anguish of these people and to respond through our witness and service.

After the church has heard the call of this minority group, it must provide an effective ministry. Some suggestions for consideration are the following specific possibilities:

1. Make every attempt to identify where Spanish-Americans are in your community and find out some of their most pressing needs and problems.

2. Organize a task force to minister to their needs. This task force may be emphasized as working in evangelism or missions or both.

3. Establish some kind of relationship between your church and one or more Spanish-American families in your community. This could take place through visitation in their homes, setting up a kindergarten program for their children, teaching English and/or citizenship classes, sponsoring youth programs, or any other service project.

4. Initiate a program of culture and language study in your local church, school or university. Make a serious attempt to learn enough Spanish to relate meaningfully to Spanish-Americans. It is amazing how many barriers can be overcome through language!

5. Become involved in some tutoring program for children

who need help because of a language handicap. This can provide opportunities for life-long friendships with the children and their parents.

6. Find ways to cooperate with secular agencies in rendering needed social services to the poor, illiterate, and those who are ill. This can be particularly applicable when the matter of employment, job training, and re-training needs to have priority.

7. Use every possible way to share what the Lordship of Christ means to you. Try to interest the families with whom you become acquainted to attend church services and to participate in all the other church programs and activities. Make them feel welcome and accepted! If language should be a problem, consider the possibility of starting a "mission" church or church school in the Spanish language either in your church or using some other available facility in their neighborhood.

8. Find strategic locations (hospitals, market places, etc.) for wide distribution of good literature printed in Spanish, such as THE UPPER ROOM, Gospel portions published by the American Bible Society, and helpful leaflets published by TIDINGS or other publishers. You may request these materials by writing to the address given below.

9. Organize a program of recreational, social and athletic activities for the youth of your community such as Scouts, Saturday night youth programs including films and games, and organized sports.

10. If your church is located in an area where there are no Spanish-Americans and would like to explore the possibility of supporting program of bilingual ministries, or if you would like additional information regarding any of the above mentioned possibilities, write the Department of Bilingual Ministries, General Board of Evangelism, 1908 Grand Avenue, Nashville, Tennessee 37203.

Victor Hugo said: "More powerful than an army with banners, is an idea whose time has come." It is my firm conviction that the idea of a relevant ministry to Hispanic-Americans is one of those ideas!

12

Membership Cultivation Through Holy Communion

by HAROLD ROGERS

In the First United Methodist Church, San Diego, California, the three services of Holy Communion are numbered among the high points of the year. Where church attendance normally shows a decrease on Communion Sunday this church has an increase of from three hundred to five hundred worshipers on these days.

The reason for the increase, according to the Rev. Charles A. McClain, pastor, and Miss Cynthia Miller, recent chairman of the Commission on Membership and Evangelism, is the visitation outreach of the church emphasized just prior to the Communion Sundays, which are observed in January, May and October.

With a membership of more than 2,800 members, this church is located near several freeways and is five miles from downtown San Diego. It has been estimated that one of the freeways which passes directly in front of the church carries an average of 85,000 cars daily.

"This is an easy church to reach by automobile," Miss Miller explained, "yet it has a very real drawback because the members of the congregation are spread out for miles in all directions and in this day of mobility they move like ants."

Under such circumstances it is very easy for members to become lost from the church, it was emphasized by those who are in close touch with the situation.

To deal with such a mobile membership a master list has been prepared and all members of the church are now listed according to the postal zone in which they reside. The city is divided into twenty-seven postal zones, consequently the church uses the same zoning system. The zones are further divided into

Harold Rogers is the Director of Discipleship Cultivation for the General Board of Evangelism of The United Methodist Church.

districts with captains who are responsible for from five to seven persons or families who are their neighbors. At the present time, over two hundred captains are required to adequately work this plan.

Communion Cards are designed to be used by visitors to invite persons to the services at First Church. The cards provide an easy point of contact between visitor and prospect. They also provide a record of attendance at the Holy Communion services.

THIS IS YOUR HOLY COMMUNION RECORD

Please write in the names of any additional members of your family attending the Holy Communion Service.

FIRST UNITED METHODIST CHURCH

2111 Camino del Rio
San Diego
California 92110

USHERS WILL COLLECT THIS CARD DURING SERVICE

In explaining how the Communion Cards are distributed and used, Miss Miller said that the captains are given their cards two Sundays prior to the Communion Service.

The captains are told, "It is not enough that we receive new members in the 'front' door of the church. We lose an alarmingly large percentage of people out the 'back door.' These people were sincere when they united with the church. Something happened! The church is a place of development. We are responsible to God for doing all within our power to make the most out of the people, who under his grace, come to worship and to work with us."

While this method has been designed primarily to encourage participation in the services of Holy Communion, other benefits have resulted and many friendships have been formed because of the visitation. Miss Miller cited the example of two retired school teachers who met and became fast friends because one had delivered a Communion Card to the other.

*Directions - list the last name of each family in left column. Place a check mark in any column if needed. Return in the envelope next Sunday to the church office.

	1	2	3	4	5

1.) Moved (get new address if possible)

2.) Need of food or clothing

3.) If there is despondency, sickness

4.) Fault found with the church or a spiritual problem

5.) Desire call by pastor

Date for Communion Sunday _____

DIRECTIONS FOR DISTRICT CAPTAINS

1. Your envelope contains a report form and the Communion Cards for your district.

2. Please list the last name of each family in the left hand column before you begin your deliveries.

3. Deliver the Communion Cards to these families during the week preceding the Communion Service. Leave the cards with an urgent request that they be present for this service. You do not need to enter the home -- calls should be brief.

4. Ask your people to bring their cards to the service. They are to use them instead of the 'I AM HERE' cards.

5. Notify the church of any situation in the home that needs attention. Do this by placing a check mark on the report form opposite their name only if any of these apply:

    a) Moved (try to obtain new address)
    b) Need of food or clothing
    c) If there is despondency, illness
    d) Fault found with the church or a spiritual problem
    e) Desire a call by the pastor

6. Return the report form in your envelope to the church office on Communion Sunday.

Remember that in doing this important service you are a representative of the church. It is not enough that we receive new members in the 'front' door of the church. We lose an alarmingly large percentage of people out the 'back' door. These people were sincere when they united with the church. Something happened! The church is a place of development. We are responsible to God for doing all within our power to make the most out of the people who, under his grace, come to worship and to work with us.

Perhaps one of the unique features about this outreach program is the fact that the captains are instructed when delivering the cards not to go into the home. Rather they present the card which bears the person's name at the door and invite that one to sign the card and bring it with him or her to the service and present it there as a record of attendance.

During this brief interview the visitor is also asked to ascertain when possible if the person is about to move, if there is a need for food or clothing, if there is despondency or sickness, if fault is found with the church, or if there is a spiritual problem or a desire to have the pastor call.

At the conclusion of the visit, report sheets provided for this purpose, are completed and returned to the church to be used as a guide for the necessary follow-up.

Those who are engaged in this outreach program are quick to emphasize that this is far more than just an attempt to get persons to attend church on a few given occasions during the year. This is a growing church in a mobile community, and this is only one of the many ways in which it tries to relate persons to it as they face daily the challenges of the world in which they live.

13

Go to the Fair

by JOE HALE

Now, as I said the way to the Celestial City lies just through this town, where this lusty fair is kept; and he that will go to the City, and yet not go through this town must need go out of the World. The Prince of Princes himself, when here, went through this Town to his own Country, and that upon a fair-day too. . . .

John Bunyan in *Pilgrim's Progress* indicated that when the visitors arrived at "Vanity Fair" they created a hub-bub for three reasons: First, their clothes were different and outlandish. Second, their speech was strange, "Because naturally," as Bunyan put it, "they spoke the language of Canaan," and third, the pilgrims "set very lightly by all their wares, and cared not so much as to look at them." If they were called on to buy, they put their fingers in their ears and cried, "Turn away mine eyes from beholding vanity; and looked upward signifying that their trade and traffic was in heaven."

Vanity Fair was a thing to be shunned.

We want to view the Fair somewhat differently—as an opportunity to be seized! For we believe the Prince of Princes visits the fair and through His presence there is a clue to the meaning of life. Here the gospel writer describes his alternative approach:

On the last and greatest day of the festival
Jesus stood and cried aloud; If anyone is thirsty,
let him come to me and whoever believes in me
let him drink.

If the Prince of Princes is present at the fair, then we follow him there.

I. *Getting Started*

How does a fair ministry develop? How is it that Christians go to a fairground to attempt to add another dimension to the fair itself? This happens because *individuals take initiative.* I

Joe Hale is Director of Ecumenical Evangelism for the General Board of Evangelism of The United Methodist Church. He holds degrees from Asbury College and Perkins School of Theology, Southern Methodist University. He is the author of *Design for Evangelism* published by Tidings. The article included here is a reflection on the author's experiences in a unique ministry.

think of a layman like Ernie Logan, who took the initiative to present a Christian witness at the Kansas State Fair, or a town pastor, Dowain McKiou, who dreamed of a potential ministry at the nearby Duquoin State Fair, a regional fair in Illinois. At Hemisfair, a world's fair in San Antonio, the initiator was a concerned and creative pastor, Paul Perry, whose interest focused in the area of unconventional evangelism. Howard West, a church administrator in Nebraska laid the groundwork for a ministry with youth at the Nebraska State Fair. In each case some interested person seized the initiative to act, and then convinced others of the need to respond to the challenge.

II. *Where Are the Opportunities?*

The opportunities are wherever people gather, at any size fair, from a world's fair like the New York Fair or Hemisfair, to regional fairs like the Duquoin State Fair, to county fairs. The number of county fairs in the United States runs into the thousands! The opportunity for a "fair ministry" is not so distant as a beach five hundred miles from your home, but in your own country! The fair is the world squeezed into a capsule form. Wherever people gather there is the opportunity to identify the One "who went through the fair and that on a fair day too."

III. *Christian Presence Identified*

Creative identification at the fair is an important element. We have learned this from previous fair attempts. In Palm Springs, California, I was once involved in a ministry to vacationing youth during the Easter season. There were two separate groups of Christians working in this setting. One group was present when we arrived. They were headquartered in the Chi Chi Club, which they had rented. They featured entertainment programs every night. Yet in a "Christian nightclub" setting they were reluctant to identify on the marquee *who* they were. They advertised on the marquee as a nightclub program, a floor show. They got the people in, closed the doors and following the entertainment gave them a message they had not expected! Only on the inside did they identify themselves. Some youth who came were angry and felt they had been trapped.

Our group had another type of identity problem. We couldn't decide *who* we were! We were in Palm Springs to have a ministry, but morning after morning, we "strategized and rationalized" until Easter week was gone and still we had little solidarity as a group. We learned a lesson for future attempts.

In a fair ministry, creative identification is crucial. The fair is a "happening." It has similarities with celebration and to this celebration of life, the Christian community adds the element of depth and reflection. To identify your program, a provocative Christian symbol is important.

In relation to this, the facilities that you find or create will determine your limitations in a fair ministry. Hemisfair provided ideal facilities. We were present as an official part of the fair. A complex of buildings known as Project-Y, for "Youth" or "You," was turned over to us for a week. There was a pop decorated theater, an open air forum, a hall left to be decorated, and a cabaret, complete with stage and lighting. To have a facility like this is highly unusual.

Generally you start from scratch in developing a facility to meet your needs. At the Duquoin State Fair the committee bought a space on the midway, built a platform, erected a tent for showing films, and built a rack for display use.

The Lutheran Church came up with the idea of building a platform decorated as an oxcart on the main thoroughfare at Hemisfair. Here they presented brief dramas at stated intervals during the day. An excellent sound system, built into the platform provided neck microphones for each actor and enhanced the flexibility to this ministry.

The symbol of the *ICHTHUS* or fish has been used in several fairs. Visible identification of your platform provides a clue and may draw people into participation through questions. Youth may wear symbolic medallions. The individual symbols designed for Hemisfair were $3\frac{1}{2}$ inches in diameter. On the face was embossed a "fish," with a small cross making the eye of the fish. On the back was printed: "Participant, IXOUE/Team, Hemisfair 1968."

This cost some money but it was a good investment. The youth who wore these medallions were easy to identify. They were present at the fair with some self-understanding and self-identity, to saturate the fairground with the symbolic suggestion of their message. The symbol became a vehicle of communication through curiosity.

IV. *Training of Participants*

At Hemisfair six hundred youth were involved during an eight day period. When you have that many persons engaged in a program it is essential that those who are doing the strategizing, are clear on their aims and procedures. Every morning, beginning with breakfast, we met for two hours to make sure we understood our assignment for that day. At Hemisfair the youth participants came at 10:00 A.M. On a given day five different youth groups from various parts of Texas might be involved. This meant a total of fifty or more participants. Two hours in training were important in helping the youth have some sense of what the day of witness was to mean and how they were to fit into the picture.

The training took place in a number of ways.

We were aware that the youth would be asking this question: "What am I to do?" Then, once they were involved after the training session ended, they would ask a second question: "Is what I am doing significant, does it matter?" If, in answer to that second question, they should react negatively, their involvement could do more harm than good.

We attempted to cultivate within the participants a sense of mission, for we felt that this could be the greatest day in their lives.

A young man came to the Duquoin Fair in Illinois with a rock and roll band. It was an excellent band and often they played in the area around Duquoin for respectable fees. This day they gave their time. At the close of the day, the young man said, "I spent only a $1.75 today but this has been the greatest day in my life!" Coupled with the opportunity of witness at a fair, there are people who are wanting to break out of the four walls of the church to creatively encounter the world and relate to it. The impact of such a venture can be impressive in their lives. We often dismiss lightly the little things that people remember. A seemingly insignificant occurrence can be a focal point in the life of an individual. The potential in a contact made at the fair is beyond our measuring.

V. *Finding Suitable Methods*

I mention ten means of ministry that have been employed at fairs. Each of these methods can be refined and the list is by no means exhaustive.

1. *Music* is a crucial media for communication at a fair. The sound needs to be suited to the occasion. This may involve a contrast. It is important to match the mood to what is appropriate to the fair scene. A church choir may not communicate at the fair singing the Sunday morning anthem! The recently popular song, "O Happy Day, When Jesus Washed My Sins Away" made the nation's "top ten." When the Edwin Hawkins Singers appeared on the Dick Clark television show they were robed and looked like an ordinary church choir, but their beat was "commercial" and it would be in keeping with the mood of the fair. So if you use a choir, be sure they can swing with the occasion. There are numerous musical possibilities: big

sound vocal groups, trumpet trios, instrumentalists, and many others.

2. *Graffiti.* The essential idea is to put up a board and let people write or draw what they want on it. At the Hemisfair our facilities included an entire room left to be decorated by the youth. This became the "Hall of Issues." David Williams of the American Bible Society helped develop this into a ministry. He drew persons into the Hall getting them involved in writing their concerns on the wall.

3. *Films.* The use of films can be an engaging part of a fair ministry. At most fairs, facility-wise you start with a vacant lot. A place to show films has to be created. At Hemisfair, an air conditioned pop-decorated theater was available but the norm is more like Duquoin where we had a tent. Since many people are suspicious about the church and religion, the accessibility of a film is important. An open-air showing on a screen or blank wall could be considered. We used the twenty-three minute film *Parable* periodically. Sometimes the attendance was just a handful; at other times there were fifty people. One carnival worker came to see it three times and after the third showing said to the coordinator, "Why, I think I get the point. I think I see what it is all about." When the film has ended it is important that people are free to leave if they desire. Discussion could begin sixty seconds later for those who would like to stay. It should be brief and discussion leaders should avoid over-explaining the films.

4. *Drama.* Drama is another method that can have a place in fair ministries. Cuttings of plays, if they are no longer than two or three minutes; fast moving skits; readings. This ministry requires a good sound system, and the right timing in presentation. If people are in a hurry to go to some other part of the fair, the time is wrong. Choose a time when the pace is slow.

5. *On-Site Presentations* can be another part of a fair ministry. These have to be negotiated with fair officials. The On-Site productions sometimes began with the group getting together to write a skit that would communicate their concerns. One afternoon eight youth went across a fairground carrying a huge sign with the word "CONCERNMENT" written on it. (I don't even know if there is such a word in the dictionary.) They had developed a skit that was simply tremendous. If the script had been prepared and handed to them, they might have been disinterested. Their skit went over big guns because they did it themselves. It made people stop and listen.

6. *Feature Productions.* How do you gather people on a fair midway or draw them closer to your platform? For this pur-

pose you need a feature presentation, something that can be performed that will bring the group together. In one such presentation, a magician performed the levitation illusion with the girl floating in mid-air. A thousand people stood by to see this, then the magician said, "Some people try to live by magic. You can't do it. Magic is for the stage! It will not work in life." At the Hemisfair, I performed a strait jacket escape from a crane seventy feet above the fairground. This is something I used to do professionally. I would not have performed otherwise simply to provide a gimmick. In other words, the difference in a "gimmick" and in doing something that is authentic is that you know what you are doing. I happen to know magic, even though I do not practice it now. After escaping from the restraint I made this statement:

> Many of you have just seen the United States Pavilion film. It is talking about life as it is. Houdini became famous because he escaped. Many years ago there was a man whose place was fixed in history because he chose not to escape!

> He wanted above all else to do the will of his Father—God. He held out his hand to help people . . . he drew it back bruised and bleeding. He was an enemy of indifference and the status quo. Those he encountered were disturbed because he told them about God. He took all the risk to live life fully.

> Finally in Jerusalem he was put to death—on a cross. But, the God he proclaimed was faithful . . . he put his stamp of approval on this man. After three days he raised him from the dead! He lives today . . . this man, Jesus Christ, makes all of life different for me! He offers to you, not a way to escape from life, but the power to live it to the full!

Such a feature production can bring an audience together.

7. *Literature.* The offering of Christian literature is a valid ministry at a fair. People pick up everything that is free at the fair. They go to the farm booth and pick up material on tractors. They will accept your material although they won't look at it in your presence. They will just drop it in a bag or in their pocket and hopefully peruse it more carefully when they get home. Do not pass out literature indiscriminately. Always establish a relationship with the people and then offer it to them. By carrying two or three pieces of material in your pocket, you can say after talking with a person, "This booklet is a favorite of mine. I don't know what meaning it will have for you, but if you are interested I would like to share it with you." If they remember you favorably, they will read the piece! A literature table can be set up at which people pick up materials.

In my judgment it is more effective for a few people to have selected pieces that they offer on a discriminate basis.

8. *Art.* Art and artists are another communication entrée at a fair. The next time you go to a fair notice where the crowd gathers on the midway. They invariably surround the artists doing caricatures. Or, they will crowd about artists doing portraits. Here is a powerful media of communication. Have a fast-working artist draw pictures that make a Christian witness. Secondly, you may develop an immobile display. Fine art reproductions are available on a loan basis from the National Gallery of Art in Washington. In a rural setting, this is more appropriate than at a place like Hemisfair.

9. *Sunday Worship Services.* At some fairs, on Sunday morning, a service has been planned specifically for the fair workers. If this is attempted, care must be taken to choose a time that will be convenient for the audience you hope to reach. Also, the response will depend largely on personal invitations being extended to the workers.

10. *Team Evaluation.* At Hemisfair, the closing time together for the team was important, so that after the activities of the day were ended at 8:00 each night the group came together and shared what the day had meant to them. At this time, the total effort seemed to fall in place as each participant reflected on his experiences with the entire team.

VI. *Principles for Fair Ministries*

1. *Work for ecumenical sponsorship.* If this is not possible, encourage ecumenical participation. It is a mistake to identify any fair witness as "United Methodist," "Southern Baptist," or "Presbyterian," for this will appear to be proselyting. If one single denomination attempts this, persons will say, "There are the Methodists doing their thing!" Why not do everything possible to make a broad Christian witness? Some of the examples to which I have referred were denominationally sponsored but ecumenical in participation.

2. *Create an approach that will be representative* of the wide range of human experience. No single method or theological stance is broad enough to encompass the fair scene. Graphics, films, drama, music, literature are appropriate vehicles for such an approach.

3. *Relate the message through personal contact.* A fair is impersonal. But when someone attends a fair and meets another who is personally interested in him, he leaves with that experience underscored in his mind. Inanimate displays are, by and large, a waste of money. They may appeal to some church-

oriented persons who will look for this kind of thing, but your primary audience will miss them.

4. *Let the medium bear the message, but stand ready to speak directly and without apology.* All will be asking this question: "Will he try to communicate on my terms or his?" The effectiveness of the encounter will depend in large part on sensitivity to this question.

5. *Involve large groups of Christian youth.* Youth are the best communicators, with appeal to both peers and adults. Allow them freedom in the form of expression they choose to utilize. Support them in what they *can* do. Let them feel their contribution is significant.

6. *Recognize the three foci of the ministry at a fair:*
   A. What happens to the participant. The importance of training.
   B. The contacts made on the fairground. This focus should be broad enough to include *both* fair workers and the attenders.
   C. The ministry of telling the story of what the individual experienced, shared, and learned at the fair to his own church and community.

7. *Make the media employed reflect the occasion.* Ferris wheels, flashing lights, surging crowds, grandstand races, fast moving exhibits—all of these are indicators of the mood of the fair. Make good use of color, movement, novelty and secular approaches.

8. *Plan to be involved at the peak periods in the fair* such as Labor Day weekend, the opening day, or the closing weekend. If the fair is held in the summer, plan an entire four to six-day period scheduling large numbers of youth to be engaged each day. If some of the youth can participate on successive days, they should be made leaders and trainers for various events and thus be integrated into the leadership.

9. *Buy the best space* rather than attempting to get the fair board to donate a spot for a religious program. You are then entering the secular community on its own terms. Create your own facility. This is better than trying to make an adaptation of something that is inadequate for your purposes or in a bad location. Seek a well-traveled intersection or main street. Design the sound system, platform, tent, pavilion, or other facilities to meet your presentation needs.

10. *Be willing to risk.* Some persons in the church will not like what you do because they believe every fair is "vanity fair." Secondly, you take a risk that people may not respond. They may ignore you—the greatest rejection of all! Thirdly, you risk,

when you open your mouth for Jesus Christ in a society in which 75 per cent of the people believe that religion is losing its influence. The question is, can we demonstrate the difference between dead religion, which we have in abundance, and vital Christian faith?

Will *you* dare offer in a secular setting a vital faith that has life-changing potential for individuals and for our society?

> The Prince of Princes himself, when here,
> went through this town into his own country,
> and that upon a fair-day too. . . .

14

Where the Action Is

by EMERSON S. COLAW

II CORINTHIANS 4:5-17; 5:17–6:1

"It was the worst of times; it was the best of times!" With this arresting phrase Charles Dickens began *The Tale of Two Cities*. It is also descriptive of God's action in human history. In Matthew's Gospel we read, "Now when Jesus was born in Bethlehem of Judea in the days of Herod the king. . . ." (2:1) Herod murdered his own wife, his mother-in-law, and assassinated three sons. Herod put infant children to the sword without hesitation. But during the reign of such a king, Christ was born! When the sixteenth century dawned it was the worst of times. Ecclesiastical office was sold to the highest bidder and the sacraments were dispensed for a price. But then the best of things happened. Martin Luther, that man of radical obedience, appeared. The Reformation had these characteristics: It was a rejection of the sacramental system and an insistence upon personal relationship with God. It gave a new emphasis to the laity which brought about marked changes both in the mode and the meaning of worship. Authority was transferred from the hierarchical structures of the church to a historic reading and understanding of the Scripture. Luther also gave an ethical system that depended not upon outward regulation but inward motivation. Drawing upon the Augustinian phrase, he said "Love God, and do as you please."

There was a sense in which the eighteenth century was the worst of times for the church. The churches were empty and the clergy generally decadent. Then the heart of John Wesley was strangely warmed.

Wesley emphasized the Reformation idea of personal relationship with God. Every Methodist preacher enjoys recounting the events of May 24, 1738. On that day Wesley rose early,

Emerson S. Colaw is pastor of Hyde Park Community United Methodist Church in Cincinnati, Ohio. He is a member of the General Board of Evangelism of The United Methodist Church and the author of *Christ's Imperatives* published by Beacon Hill Press. The article included here is a portion of a sermon delivered at the 1969 meeting of the United Methodist Council on Evangelism.

as was his custom, and resorted to Scripture. The passage which caught his attention was prophetic for it spoke of the fulfillment of the promised kingdom. In the afternoon he went to St. Paul's Cathedral, that magnificent edifice conceived, designed and brought to completion by Sir Christopher Wren. There he heard a choir of superb technical competence sing an anthem based upon the Psalm, "Out of the depths have I cried unto Thee." And while the Psalm could match his mood, it did not correct it. In the evening he went to Aldersgate Street. In our preaching we frequently stop with the experience of the warm heart but if we read on we discover that after the moment of exaltation he fell to his knees and began to pray for his enemies. He was then escorted in triumph by a group of his friends to the quarters of his brother Charles, and burst in upon him with the exclamation, "I believe, I believe." They fell into one another's arms, as would have been characteristic of that day, and then began to sing together a hymn which Charles had earlier composed. One line of it went, "O, how shall I the goodness tell which thou to me hast shown?" The burden of Wesley's life from that day forward was to do precisely that.

He also used the laity in a fresh and responsible way. The Methodist movement was largely a lay effort. He also articulated an ethical system that did not depend upon the crutches of rules. We have often assumed that the doctrine of Christian perfection is concerned with a subjective emotional experience. Even as Luther gave new expression to an ethical system that was based not upon outward regulation but inward motivation, so Wesley's doctrine of Christian perfection was concerned with the same issue. He was calling us, in his statements about perfection, not to pursue an impossible ideal. He was urging man to be free from slavish obedience to rules and to live a life of such communion with God that the natural fruit of this relationship would be righteousness and holiness.

In addition to the Reformation emphases, Wesley brought the dimension of mission to the work of the church. Soon after his Aldersgate experience, Wesley was meeting with a small group of friends in the old Foundry in London. An invitation came from George Whitefield to come to Bristol and take up the ministry of preaching in the open air. Wesley was as bewildered and repelled by that invitation as most of us would be. He did not know what to do with it, so submitted it to the little group with whom he was meeting in the Foundry. On that slender thread hung the future of the Methodist Church. They voted that he should go. His true feeling is represented by the fact that he wrote, "I submitted myself to be more vile." He went to

Bristol, preached in the open air, and to his astonishment the Spirit of God was there. He later recorded that the colliers who listened were so moved by the grace of God that the tears coursing down their cheeks left white rivulets in the coaldust. From that time forward Wesley was the prophet of the long road!

His activities, however, were not limited to preaching. He was forever at the job of combating all those things that destroyed the dignity and worth of man. The Grog Shop and child labor were among the enemies he fought.

The phrase, "It was the worst of times; it was the best of times!" may also apply to our moment in history. Innumerable books and articles are suggesting that this may be the worst of times for the church. The ministry is in a muddle, we are told. We are the last of the "generalizers" in an age of specialization and therefore we are fragmented. Joe Sittler refers to it as "The maceration of the minister." We are frustrated by committee meetings, budget making, program planning, and the inevitable criticism. We are haunted by the fear that the battles to which we are giving energy may finally prove to be irrelevant. Little wonder that one of our bishops has said the major problem confronting him in the administration of his episcopal office is ministerial morale.

The contemporary church is also characterized by theological confusion. Protestantism has traditionally affirmed a transcendent God, uniquely revealed in Jesus Christ, knowledge of whom may be obtained by a historic reading and understanding of the Scripture. But the works of such men as Bishop Robinson, Thomas Altizer, and William Hamilton signal an erosion of theological certainty.

The validity of the institutional church is under debate. The works of such men as Pierre Berton, Peter Berger, Gibson Winter and many others raise serious doubts as to whether the church can any longer be a redemptive instrument. Indicative of this new trend of thinking is an illustration used by Dudley Ward in his volume, *Secular Man in Sacred Mission* published by Tidings. He tells the story of a Jesuit priest who went as a missionary to India. He spent fifteen or twenty years helping the farmers. Then a reporter from a Catholic paper came to talk with him. The reporter said, "I suppose there have been many conversions."

And the priest answered, "Oh yes, many conversions. The farmers are now doing better, some in fact have even become rich."

The reporter persisted, "I mean, many of them have joined the church."

The priest thought for a moment and then slowly said, "Well . . . well no, none have joined the church."

A little impatiently now, the reporter said, "But they are attending church."

And the Father answered, "No, as a matter of fact I have been so busy living and planting God in this area that I myself have not been to church for eighteen months." Mr. Ward adds, "This is a new dimension in religious witness in our age."

The fourth characteristic of our day, as I would see it, is an astonishing lack of any overwhelming sense of commitment and loyalty on the part of the laity. We were doing a little work with our non-resident membership list not too long ago and I wrote a letter to one family that had been very active in our church. A letter came back from the woman and it read something like this: "Mr. Colaw, we now live near a university campus and we go every Sunday morning to the chapel service there. They have unusually fine music provided by the university personnel; they have nationally known preachers every Sunday morning." And she added the note which I didn't think necessary, "We had not heard preaching such as this before." She said, "The children are taught in Sunday School by seminary students." But then she concluded, "But best of all there is no membership, no pledging and no Woman's Society asking me to work. So if you don't mind we'll just leave our membership at Hyde Park and continue to enjoy what we have here." Now I think this is representative of no overwhelming sense of commitment to the faith.

After the 1968 General Conference in Dallas we had a little static in Cincinnati. A newspaper carried a headline which read, "Methodist Group Endorses Right to Disobey Law." Now if you read all the story I think it was a fairly accurate presentation of what happened at Dallas. One of our families wrote a letter asking that their membership be discontinued. I went to see them. This very fine woman, a member of the DAR, very bluntly said to me, "My country is more important to me than my church."

In the light of this it is little wonder that ministers in unprecedented numbers are surrendering their credentials and seem prepared to abandon the church and permit it to be absorbed by the world. And yet, if we understand the historical record, in the worst of times God is at work preparing the best.

I think great things have happened. Because of the ecumenical movement we are enjoying a new kind of freedom.

Great gains have come to us out of church renewal. We simply have to accept the idea that if we are going to have ministers and laymen who are really committed, then there will be a falling away of nominal members.

But we live in an age of unusual opportunity and we must affirm, if the record of history is right, that the worst of times is also the best of times. Now I am not here to sell you on the glories of the local church. You are all far too experienced and hard-nosed for that kind of thing. A couple years ago one of our colleagues had an article in *The Christian Advocate* in which he was talking about the ministry and ended up by saying, "I would rather be the pastor of a local United Methodist Church than anything else known to man." Well, I feel committed to the ministry, but I am not often moved to that ecstatic utterance. But let me share certain convictions and as I share these convictions it is in the knowledge that no one man can speak to all of us. We are too diverse, we are too complicated, and if there is someone who has given up on the local church, then what I have to say may fall on deaf ears. I know that. But I dare hope that most of you would share these convictions.

First, I am convinced that God will not be without a witness. Now that witness may not bear the label of The United Methodist Church. All forms and structures are temporal, but the eternal truth will prevail. I must hold to that conviction.

The second conviction is that the church, defined, not as an ecclesiastical organization, but as the "community of believers," will be preserved to the end of time.

Third, this fellowship organized for study, worship, and action is essential for the realization of God's kingdom.

Now phrases such as, "the invisible Christ," and "religionless Christianity," which we usually assume means Christianity without organization, when carried to their final conclusions, betray the Christian gospel by an eclecticism which mutes personal belief and leaves mankind without a universal Christ as Savior and Lord.

With this background, let us turn to the examination of the areas of action. My purpose is to examine the traditional disciplines as areas of action. Start with the Reformation emphasis upon personal relationship with God, for this is what *worship* is all about. In one of his volumes Camus has a great insight: "This is what frightens me, to see the sense of this life dissipated, to see our reason for existence disappear. This is intolerable. A man cannot live without a reason."

In worship, as a man confronts the holiness of God, he discovers the meaning of his life. I know that many of our worship services are fundamentally dull, inglorious, and lacking in abrasive. I am not sure that it need be that way and we ought to be experimenting.

One of my successors in a church where I once served has quite a flare for this kind of thing, and in his first service there, he arranged that in the middle of the worship hour balloons would start dropping down. That congregation really must have been startled. But he explained, "Now by way of illustration this symbolizes that when our life is spirit-filled there ought to be a joy and a bounce about us." Well, this is his way of doing it. That would not be authentic for me.

Dr. Elson, of National Presbyterian Church, in an article on worship, described a well-structured service with its moods and movements such as adoration, confession, forgiveness, instruction, dedication, etc. He then concluded by asking, "Where is there a greater astringent and healing power in the world? Where also is the dynamic for action in the secular order if it is not found in the gospel of the crucified and risen Christ? Where else is humanity to be made aware of its oneness except in God's family?"

For some years I served in Chicago and while there Jerry Walker was serving the old St. James Church, on the South Side, right in the midst of the slums. A church of distinguished history, it had given two bishops to the church. Then Jerry wrote an article. In the article he describes the vital force that the church provided in his neighborhood:

"Where God was placed above man and love of man was an imperative stemming from love and worship of God, the institution renewed itself and became a growing force in the renewal of the community."

When all the innovations have been tried and all the new theories promoted there will still be a need for the people of God to join together in worship, thus equipping themselves for their ministries.

This brings me to my second thought. Luther emphasized the laity, Wesley emphasized the laity. I think one of the hopeful signs right now is the emergence of the laity. They are going to retreat centers, they are involved in discussion and Bible study groups in our churches. We have seen new life in their midst. Ephesians 4:12 says, "We are to be pastors and teachers." It's tied together with an "and" "pastors and teachers, to equip God's people for work in his service." Now the phrase "equipping ministry" provides an exciting image of what the professional clergy might be doing. One author writing on church renewal has these lines, "The idea of the pastor as the equipper is one

which is full of promise, bringing back self-respect to men in
the ministry when they are solely discouraged by conventional
patterns."

Well, our author is saying, "Here is a job which is as intrinsically hard as the job of the official prayer at banquets is
intrinsically easy." To watch for undeveloped powers, to draw
them out, to bring potency to actuality in human lives, this is a
self-validating task. A man who knows that he is performing
such a function is not bothered by problems of popular acceptance, because he is working at something he can respect.
He is saved from triviality for he knows that his work is both
necessary and important. In other words, he is a discoverer, the
developer and the trainer of the powers of other men.

This is the meaning of the Biblical terminology "equipping
ministry." Now let's face it. We need a tough new breed of
servant-minded pastors who are willing to lose their lives in
building up the ministries of their people. Of all the church
renewal books I have read, the one by Wallace Fisher, *From
Tradition to Mission,* is the one which spoke best to me. He
devotes considerable space to a discussion of his work with the
ninety "under-shepherds," giving time to the core group who,
in turn became ministers to the rest of the congregation. When
we use the "priesthood of all believers" as a phrase, let's remember this: it does not mean that every man can do as he
pleases or believe as he wishes. It means each of us has a responsibility to minister to our brother.

Third, the Reformation found its authority in a historic reading and interpretation of the Word, and today's preacher is to
set forth the Word of God. Now preaching may be obsolete as
we are often told, but the fact remains that congregations still
gather on Sunday morning. Preaching is still one of those in-
struments which we are using, so we must find ways of making
it valid.

Helmut Thielicke, in his volume, *The Trouble with the Church,*
says, "Wherever we find, even in this day, a vital living congregation, we find at its center vital preaching." Good preaching
is still possible and it can make a crucial difference. People will
gather where they have a reasonable expectation that they will
hear some vital issue presented with clarity and conviction.
The largest crowds that gather in our city, apart from sports
events, gather to hear a speaker.

If you go into the west entrance of Westminster Abbey you
encounter a very simple plaque which reads, "Remember
Winston Churchill." Twenty-nine years ago, when the bombs
were falling on London, the nation of England was in a state

of shock, Winston Churchill stood up and by the force of his
eloquence rallied a people to do battle and win ultimate
victory. And only a few years ago the American people were
electrified when John F. Kennedy stood on the steps of the
Capitol and cried, "Ask not what your country can do for you."
Preaching can identify issues; preaching can mobilize a response.
    Now what do we preach about? We preach about God and his
claim upon us. Elton Trueblood says, "My life almost exactly
parallels the 20th century." Trueblood is now 68. He continues,
"I have watched three movements come. First, the missionary
movement when Robert Speer and John R. Mott gathered thousands of college young people in convocations and laid upon
them the claim of missions. Then came the ecumenical movement
reaching its climax at Amsterdam in 1948. The last fifteen
years we have seen church renewal and how grateful we are for
what it has brought to the church."
    But, in his judgment, he says, "The force of these three move-
ments has been spent." No one gets very excited now about
ecumenicity. *The Christian Century* in an editorial analyzing
the decade of the '60's, said no one is particularly dismayed by
the failures of COCU, and no one is excited about its promise
because it really doesn't matter that much.
    Where is the new movement to go? What's going to be the
next thing that captures us? Trueblood says that in his judgment, it will be an era of radical belief in God, because we sud-
denly realize we must get back to foundations. So we must preach
about God and his claim upon life.
    I think the day will also come when we will regret our ab-
dication of responsibility as a church to give moral guidance.
I have tried to state rather clearly what I understand here in
this area of an ethical system that does not depend upon rules,
but we do have responsibility for giving guidelines to our generation.
    A social worker was recently speaking to a group and she told
about spending a year and a half helping a boy learn to walk.
Then she said, "Where do you think that boy is now?" Well
there were various guesses, such as the ministry, or a lawyer,
etc. She said, "No, he is in prison on death row for murder."
Then she said, "I was so busy teaching him how to walk I didn't
take time to teach him where to walk."
    Preaching must also be personal witness. Some years ago
when in Chicago I went to Music Hall to hear Chuck Templeton,
the Canadian Evangelist who had left a brilliant career in television. He had an amazing ability for communication and I
listened with great appreciation. On the shelf of my library is

his book *Life Looks Up*. Some time ago Chuck Templeton went
back into television and the secular press made a lot out of this.
Someone interviewed him. They said, "Why?"

With complete candor Chuck Templeton said, "Because I
ceased to believe in the divinity to Christ.[11]

I have a conviction that if a man has a living experience
of Christ he will have something to say. I believe that. Some
time ago Yale University was searching for a new president and
someone described the kind of man for whom they were looking
by saying he must be a leader, not too far to the right, not too
far to the left, and of course, not too much in the middle. He
must be a great speaker, excellent writer, a skilled public relations man and an expert fund-raiser. He must be a young man
but also mature and full of wisdom. He must be married to a
paragon, a combination of Queen Victoria, Florence Nightingale,
and the best dressed woman of the year. He must be a Yale
man, but also a scholar. He went on listing other qualifications
and when he ended he said, "Now it must be apparent that only
one has most of these qualifications, but is God a Yale man?
Unfortunately, in this barbaric world we will never know."

Now David MacLennan used that in his book to say this,
"Delete the reference to the University and you have a description of the parish ministry." I read that and I said to myself,
"Who really is equal to that?" Then I remembered we are not
expected to do all that. We are to point to Him who said, "I
am the way, the truth, and the life."

Now let me talk a moment about this matter of mission. A
time of revolution is a time of prophecy. The Archbishop of
Canterbury has a memorable phrase: "The Church exists for
the sake of those who never enter its doors."

Those of us who have an evangelistic concern must add the
element of vital love and compassion to the prophetic work of the
church. I have the feeling that it is easy to get involved in
prophecy out of hostility. But when I begin studying the life of
the prophets they were never concerned about personal abuse;
they were aroused when they saw someone being robbed of
dignity, worth and identity.

Amos was a common laborer, herding the flock, caring for the
sycamore trees, but when he saw what was happening to the
poor he went down to Bethel, mounted the steps of the Royal
Shrine and cried, "You people, look at what you are doing, listen
to God." It is an Abraham Lincoln standing in the slave mart
and saying, "If I ever get a chance to hit that, I'll hit it hard."
It's a G. Bromley Oxnam, all caught up in the administration
of an Episcopal office, beginning to see honest people, patriotic

people, harassed by the House Committee on Un-American Activities just because they were different. As his anger was stirred, he went before that committee exposing their activities to the light of day.

Martin Luther King was just a brilliant, eloquent preacher until he became angry. Mrs. Rosa Parks, weary after a day's work, was arrested because she sat down on a bus. He rose up in his anger, not at anything about himself but because he saw people being robbed of dignity and worth.

Carry the story on. A Dr. Spock, who when he saw a generation that he had helped rear being sent off to die in what he considered to be a senseless war, could not restrain himself. His anger was because of what was happening to others. The prophetic road grows out of a spirit that is compassionate and sensitive, filled with a deep love. This is, I think, our contribution to the role of prophecy in an age of revolution.

Some time ago we had Olin Stockwell in our congregation. I read his little book, *Meditations from a Prison Cell*. In one passage he told of being in a cell with a Chinese Communist. The cell mate asked if he could borrow Mr. Stockwell's blanket and Olin Stockwell said to him, "No." The cellmate had body lice and he knew if he let him use his blanket he then would have body lice. Then in this little meditation he adds: "I asked myself, what would a Christian do? And I let him have the blanket." Then he adds this line, "Body lice, like the Christian faith, is caught only by contact."

Now all around are forces robbing people of dignity and worth and identity. The church, the pulpit, and the street are places where we can go and bear our witness against those forces that destroy God's image. This is where you find the action!